Christian
COSMO

THE SEX TALK YOU *NEVER* HAD

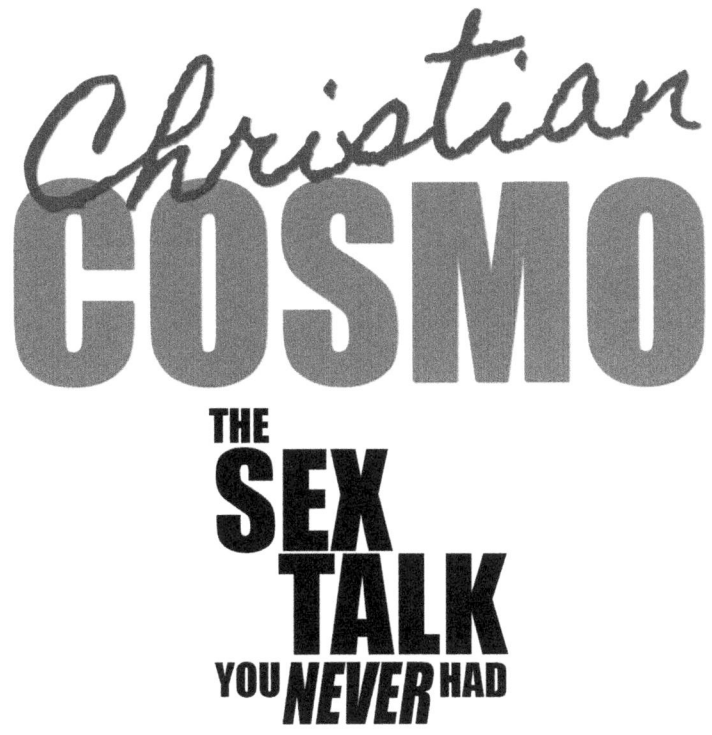

PHYLICIA MASONHEIMER

© 2017 by Phylicia Masonheimer

Cover and Interior Design by Roseanna White Designs

All rights reserved. No part of this publication may be reproduced, stored in a retrieval system, or transmitted in any form or by any means – for example, electronic, photocopy, recording – without the prior written permission of the publisher. The only exception is brief quotations in printed reviews.

ISBN: 978-1544719764

All Scripture quotations, unless otherwise indicated, are taken from the Holy Bible, New International Version®, NIV®. Copyright ©1973, 1978, 1984, 2011 by Biblica, Inc.™ Used by permission of Zondervan. All rights reserved worldwide. www.zondervan.com The "NIV" and "New International Version" are trademarks registered in the United States Patent and Trademark Office by Biblica, Inc.™

Christian Cosmo is the sex talk many girls never get. Rather than learn about sex from the culture, *Christian Cosmo* answers sexual questions from a Scriptural standpoint. By reframing sex for the single girl, we lay the foundation for God-honoring marriages and end the stigma on female sexuality.

TABLE OF CONTENTS

Introduction..9

Reclaiming Sex From the Culture..11

Reframing Sex In Your Mind...23

Why God Designed Sex for Marriage................................35

What if I'm Not a Virgin?..47

How to Live as a Forgiven Woman....................................55

Why Getting Married Won't Stop Sexual Sin....................69

What to Know About the Wedding Night.........................85

How to Overcome a Sexual History..................................93

The Truth About Fantasizing..105

Preach the Gospel With Your Sexuality...........................113

Acknowledgements..119

APPENDIX I...121

APPENDIX II..129

APPENDIX III...139

INTRODUCTION

More and more Christian girls enter adulthood with no knowledge of sex as God designed it.

I was one of those girls.

I never had a "talk" with my parents; I learned about sex from books, movies, and my friends. I figured out some more details in college and, with the help of Google, finally understood the big picture.

As a veteran of purity culture, I knew all the "rules" of sex - but I didn't understand my own sexuality. My first exposure to it was at twelve years old when I found an erotic romance at a garage sale. I hid my newfound knowledge, and by fifteen became addicted to erotica and masturbation. I learned about sex from all the wrong sources and lived out my sexuality in all the wrong ways. Because I had only ever known sex in the context of sin, and I didn't know how to see it in a positive light.

It took years for me to learn that God's design for sex was

monumentally different from the way our culture portrays it. And as I learned to embrace and celebrate my sexuality as a single woman, I honored it with the value God meant it to possess.

God's power is perfected in weakness. He redeemed my sexuality and gave both me and my husband (whose story is shared in this book) a beautiful foundation upon which to build our marriage – something we definitely did not deserve.

If I had it over, I would have loved to talk to a young, married woman who could explain sex in light of God's Word. I would have loved to get my questions answered before curiosity led to sin. Through this e-book, I hope I can be for you what I never had.

My desire is for your picture of sexuality to be reframed. I hope this book transforms your attitude toward sex, removes your fears, and inspires you to embrace the whole woman God made you to be – physically, emotionally, spiritually, *and* sexually.

In Him,

Phylicia

RECLAIMING SEX FROM THE CULTURE

It is a topic clouded in secrecy, accessible only by uttering the exclusive password: "I do." Locked out of the discussion, single women piece together a sexual worldview from parents and peers.

Sex is bad.

Sex is great.

Sex is holy.

Sex is hot.

We don't know what is true and what is false; what is cultural and what is biblical.

But not anymore.

In this book, we're going to talk about sex. No more secrets. No more assumptions. No more lies.

Sex is an intimate and valuable thing. It should be treated with reverence and respect. We struggle to discuss it because we're unsure of the line between privacy and honesty. But we desperately need a biblical, truth-focused approach to sex.

As a teenager, I knew sex existed. I wanted to know more, but I felt guilty about pursuing that knowledge. I quickly saw sex and shame as one entity. My sources for sexual information weren't that great: Cosmopolitan, Jane Magazine, and whatever articles I could find online. These offered facts about sex, but rarely did those facts coincide with my Christian worldview. I longed for truth about my sexuality; I wanted the details of Cosmo, but the perspective of Christ.

I never found what I was looking for, so now - ten years later - I'm writing it for you.

REFRAMING YOUR VIEW OF SEXUALITY

Many young women view sex through a lens of guilt and fear. In modern culture, sex is put on display and stripped of its intimacy. But in Christian circles, sex isn't talked about at all. Shrouded in mystery and ignorance, the facts of sex remain hidden until a girl "needs" them before marriage, at which point fear and doubt have already wrought havoc on her expectations. But these extremes do not need to be our reality.

Sex is not evil. It's not dirty, naughty, or bad. Sex is an amazing and beautiful thing because it was created by our amazing and beautiful God! Because God created sex, if it is used according to God's design (within marriage) there is absolutely nothing "dirty" about it! Because of this, there is no cause for shame when we talk about sex. True freedom comes as we bring it into the open, learning what God-defined sexuality looks like before *and* after marriage.

When we believe lies about sex, we cheat ourselves of the balanced, faithful stewardship God expects for our sexuality. Whether we like it or not God created us as sexual beings – even *before* marriage! Saying "I do" doesn't magically press a button that makes us sexual. How we view our sexuality *before* marriage plays a huge role in how much we enjoy it in the marriage bed. That's why it's imperative we reframe how we think about sex.

How do we do this? We start by looking at what God has to say. God said a lot about sex, not just in regard to sexual sin:

- **Our sexuality is part of our image, and we were made in the likeness of God:**
    - "So God created man in his own image, in the image of God he created him; male and female he created them." (Gen. 1:27)
- **Sex is a depiction of perfect unity:**
    - "Therefore a man shall leave his father and his mother and hold fast to his wife, and they shall become one flesh." (Gen. 2:24)
- **Sex is intensely gratifying when used within God's design:**
    - "Let your fountain be blessed, and rejoice in the wife of your youth, a lovely deer, a graceful doe. Let her

breasts fill you at all times with delight; be intoxicated always in her love." (Prov. 5:18-19)

- **Sex is exciting, fulfilling, and an expression of covenant love:**
    - "Let him kiss me with the kisses of his mouth! For your love is better than wine; your anointing oils are fragrant; your name is oil poured out; therefore virgins love you. Draw me after you; let us run." (Song 1:1-2)

- **Sex is holy and honorable:**
    - "Let marriage be held in honor among all, and let the marriage bed be undefiled..." (Heb. 13:4)

By making sex more or less than it actually is, our spiritual enemy has completely altered our approach to it - both before and after marriage.

Our sexuality is just one facet of our being, but that part of us is intrinsically connected to our minds, bodies, and spirits. Sexuality involves all the parts of who we are and as such is an incredible responsibility – but it's a responsibility worth celebrating.

HOW TO CELEBRATE YOUR SEXUALITY

We don't often hear the words "celebrate" and "sexuality" in the same sentence, particularly within the church.

Our sexual capabilities are good, holy, and beautiful. They are designed to bring glory to God (and pleasure to us) when used according to God's direction:

> *"For this is the will of God, your sanctification: that you abstain from sexual immorality; that each one of you know how to control his own body in holiness and honor, not in the passion of lust like the Gentiles who do not know God... (1 Thess. 4:3-5)*

Our sexuality is not dirty. But when used for selfish purposes, it becomes tainted by sin. When we use our sexual capabilities outside of God's design, we experience guilt and shame. The enemy leads us to believe that sex – not sin – is the source of our shame. And as long as we believe that sex is the problem, we will be blind to the real issue at hand: the spiritual war being waged against us.

By recognizing that the essence of sexuality is holy, we operate on a higher plane. We are covered by the sacrificial blood of Christ; His blood didn't just cover our eternal destiny. Christ died so we could be *wholly redeemed.* If our whole being is made new in Christ, we are indeed a new creation (2 Cor. 5:17), altogether beautiful in the eyes of God: Spiritually, physically, and sexually.

> *"...he has granted to us his precious and very great promises, so that through them you may become partakers of the divine nature, having escaped from the corruption that is in the world because of sinful desire." (2 Peter 1:4)*

Above all else, Satan is a liar. Because our sexuality affects our greatest vulnerabilities – and because it is precious to God – the enemy targets it at every opportunity. He uses the same lies over and over:

- Sex is dirty, evil, and gross.
- Your sexual sins determine who you are.
- A good man will never want you.
- God no longer loves you.

This negative perspective of sexuality causes us to see it as burdensome, wearying, shameful, and dirty. When we view sex in this light, any existing sexual sin is perpetuated by despair.

Satan's sexuality is not celebrated: it is either *hidden* or *flaunted*. His version of sex is not just a *part* of who we are – it is *all* of who we are. For some, this results in a spiral of shame and defeat. Others use their sexuality as a form of power and manipulation. Sex is either the problem or the idol, and either way, is exalted above the power of God.

Blinded from the truth by this false sexuality, many women give up or give in. But *you* don't have to.

> *"And I will give them one heart, and a new spirit I will put within them. I will remove the heart of stone from their flesh and give them a heart of flesh, that they may walk in my statutes and keep my rules and obey them. (Ezekiel 11:19)*

Lie-based sexuality burdens us with sin or selfishness. God's design brings freedom.

A positive, celebratory sexual perspective is empowering. It motivates holy living and pure choices, strengthening us against lustful desires and drawing us into fellowship with the Lord. This perspective requires that we reframe what we've been taught about our sexuality, letting go of the lies and replacing them with God's truth.

Your sexuality is not the enemy. Your body is not the enemy. Your desires are not the enemy.

Your enemy is Satan, and you are engaged in a spiritual war designed to separate you from Jesus Christ.

Sin separates us from God, and sexual sin has even greater implications:

> *"Flee from sexual immorality. Every other sin a person commits is outside the body, but the sexually immoral person sins against his own body. (1 Cor. 6:18)*

Satan comes to steal, kill, and destroy our perspective of sex. Christ came to give us abundant life (John 10:10). Our sexuality is part of our created design, and its part of our Christian lives. Therefore, it follows that our sexuality should be just as submitted to Christ as the rest of our being. Grace-driven, gratitude-focused women will use their sexuality to the glory of God because they see through Satan's lies to God's intentions.

YOUR SEXUALITY IS A GIFT

"Blessed are the pure in heart, for they shall see God. (Matthew 5:8)

To see God's will, we must be in pure fellowship with Him. This fellowship requires obedience, and obedience is built on *trust*. We sin against God because *we don't trust Him.*

Every act of disobedience is a statement: *God, you aren't enough for me.*

Whether we disobey in our finances, relationships, or sexuality, all of our actions point back to trust. If we believe God is enough – that He will provide, protect, and otherwise do everything He has promised to do in His Word – we won't take matters into our own hands.

The enemy's first lie (and the root of every lie he tells) is the same: *Did God really say...?*

Is God really enough?

Is God's plan for sex really good?

Isn't He withholding something from you?

When we rejoice in God's intentions for our sexuality, we show gratitude for His design. We evidence trust in His plan and peace with the body He has given us. Our sexuality is a gift, but when single, that fullness of that gift is relegated to a later time. **This doesn't make it any less of a gift!** By celebrating our sexuality – viewing it with positivity and joy – we embrace God's intentions for our womanhood.

True sexual freedom can't be found in what the world has to offer: Where men and women are enslaved to their own desires. Women of God handle sexual desire spiritually *first*. They are not motivated by impulse, but by goodness. They aren't asking, "How far can I go?" but "How holy can I be?"

How do we rejoice in single sexuality? How do we choose obedience? We start by thanking God for this design. We start by choosing trust in every area of life. Your sexuality is a holy and beautiful thing, and when the time is right, you will know the completeness of this gift.

RENEWED MIND, REDEEMED SEXUALITY

In order to celebrate our sexuality God's way, we have to align our minds with His Word. Many of us don't recognize the predispositions and biased perspectives we have about sex until we check our thoughts against the truth. Paul talks about this in Romans 12:2:

> *"Do not conform to the pattern of this world, but be transformed by the renewing of your mind. Then you will be able to test and approve what God's will is--his good, pleasing and perfect will."*

Renewing our minds – breaking old though patterns and replacing them with the truth – doesn't just transform the way we live. It teaches us to test ideologies against the truth. A renewed mind is aligned with an objective standard to guide us into wise decision-making and a godly perspective on sex.

We need to question the worldly portrayals of sex we see around us. This thought pattern might look something like this:

World: Men just want sex all the time, especially after marriage, when sex is boring and dutiful.

Believer: Is this cultural portrayal of sex accurate? What does God's Word say?

World: "Likewise the husband does not have authority over his own body, but the wife. Do not deprive one another, except by mutual consent for a limited time, so you may devote yourselves to prayer. Then come together again, so that Satan will not tempt you through your lack of self-control." (1 Cor. 7:4-5)

"May he kiss me with the kisses of his mouth! For your love is better than wine." (Song 1:2)

Believer: This passage in Corinthians indicates that women desire their husbands just as much as husbands desire their wives. In Song of Solomon, the bride shares her desire for her husband as much as he does for her. These cultural generalizations about sex don't apply to every marriage, and they don't have to apply to me. They are negative portrayals and I reject them from my mind.

We must make a habit of questioning what we believe about sex. By checking it against the truth of God's Word, we find freedom and healing from negative sexual perceptions.

DOES MY VIEW OF SEX REALLY MATTER?

What's the big deal with negative sexual perceptions? First, a negative view of sexuality cannot be separated from a negative view of ourselves as a whole. Sexuality is as much a part of our created being as the rest of our minds and bodies. God never said sex was dirty. God said to use it according to His design. When we treat part of our created nature as evil, we seek to suppress it rather than use it for the glory of God.

Secondly, a negative view of sexuality has the power to destroy intimacy in marriage. How we understand sex *before* marriage has a profound effect on sexual intimacy *within* the marital bond. Too often, sex is not open for discussion until right before the wedding night. This willful ignorance about God's gift of intimacy shrouds what should be a beautiful event in guilt, shame, and fear. Rather than enjoy marital sex with freedom, many young women come into marriage terrified of the unknown, unsure of what is "acceptable", unable to release the tension of fear from their minds and bodies.

Allowing God to transform our understanding of sexuality is the first step to true sexual freedom. God's sexual freedom isn't about throwing off standards of right and wrong; it's about embracing all parts of our created being and using them to draw attention to His grace. Christian sexuality is not dirty, bad, or evil. It is not stilted, prudish, or withdrawn. God's design for sex is the design of freedom: freedom to enjoy the fulfillment of covenant love. It is freedom from guilt, shame, and fear; freedom to be the woman He designed you to be.

QUESTIONS TO CONSIDER:

1. Have you viewed your sexuality as a gift or a burden? How did you come to that conclusion?

2. What steps do you need to take to transform your view of sexuality?

3. What lies do you need to reject about sex? What truths need to replace them?

REFRAMING SEX IN YOUR MIND

This might be a little awkward.

Though I frequently discuss sex on my blog, I typically glaze over the details. Unfortunately, not every young woman reading this book understands how sex works, and we can't move forward in this conversation until the details are out of the way.

Some of you already understand sex from a biological perspective, and if so, this chapter will be a review for you. For others, this chapter is necessary to complete their understanding of sexuality, particularly those whose parents never facilitated "The Talk". This chapter won't get into sexual perversions, sexual sin or struggles with lust – we'll discuss those later on. For now, we're concentrating on some basic facts and definitions.

It's difficult to talk about the "nitty gritty" of sex, but remember: God designed our sexual organs the same way He designed every other part of our bodies! Just because our sexual organs are private doesn't mean we should be embarrassed of them. They were designed with the same intricacy and care as our eyes, nose, skin, arms, and legs. All parts of our body work together *with* our reproductive system to enable an incredible sexual experience in marriage. Our senses of sight, smell, and touch are just as pivotal to sex as our sexual organs themselves.

In the following pages, I'll define some basic sexual terminology and activities. Whether this is your first "sex-ed" experience or simply a review, remember to uphold a *positive* view as you read on.

WHAT IS SEXUAL INTERCOURSE?

When people say someone "had sex", they're referencing the act of sexual intercourse. Prior to actually having sex, both the man and woman must become sexually aroused. For men, this means an increased heart rate and a rush of blood flow to the penis, which becomes "hard" and erect. At the same time, his wife also become aroused. Blood flow increases to her clitoris (the source of female sexual pleasure) and the tissue surrounding her vagina, which also swells with blood. Her body naturally lubricates her vagina, enough so for her husband's penis to enter painlessly.

When they are both ready, the husband will "penetrate" his wife and use a rhythmic motion to stimulate them both. The culmination of intercourse is orgasm, or the feeling of pleasure as one or both partners "climax". Unlike the movies, not all couples climax simultaneously. There may be times when one partner climaxes and the other does not; when both reach orgasm, but not at the same time; or when they both climax simultaneously. The longer a couple is married, the more acquainted they will become with what works for them sexually – which can result in more simultaneous climaxes. Practice makes perfect!

The husband's orgasm results in a release of semen. This is called ejaculation. If his wife is ovulating, their sexual encounter could result in pregnancy.

WHAT IS FOREPLAY?

Foreplay is used to encourage arousal prior to sexual intercourse. This could include making out, deep or "French" kissing, petting, caressing, sexy games, strip teases, and the like. All of these are meant to lead up to the sexual encounter between husband and wife. For most couples, the longer foreplay lasts the more, aroused they become and the more enjoyable the intercourse. For women, arousal usually takes longer to occur, so foreplay improves her experience. It also improves the experience for the husband, as delayed gratification can make the climax more intense.

WHAT ARE SEX POSITIONS?

Sex positions are exactly what the sound like: ways to position your body during sex. The most common position is called "missionary": husband on top, wife on her back below him. There are countless positions with which a couple can experiment, with names like 69, cowgirl, reverse cowgirl, and girl-on-top. Sometimes changing a position can make sex more enjoyable for one or both partners – especially the wife, who needs to have her clitoris stimulated to achieve orgasm. There are apps, calendars, and books available that offer different position ideas.

WHAT ARE SEX TOYS?

Sex "toys" come in many shapes and sizes. They have different purposes and uses depending on what kind of toy is in question. If used as part of foreplay and/or sex (not alone, separated from mutual intimacy) and used for consensual pleasure (NOT abuse), sex toys can find a place in Christian marriage.

Sex games are also diverse; some can be fun and simple, like strip poker (betting items of clothing instead of chips or money in the well-known card game). If the game involves sexual perversions or challenges one or both partners are uncomfortable integrating into their sexual relationship, it is wise to refrain from participating. Discernment and open discussion should always be part of a sexual relationship with your spouse.

Lingerie (my personal favorite!) may be anything from a sexy bra set to a lacy negligee to a corset with thigh-high nylons. Victoria's Secret is renowned for their merchandise in this market. There are many places to buy lingerie outside of Victoria's Secret (many Christians object to funding their obscene ad campaigns). My own favorite is AdoreMe, and Burlington Coat Factory (surprisingly) has an affordable lingerie section as well.

WHAT IS ORAL SEX?

Oral sex occurs when one partner stimulates the sexual organs of the other with his or her mouth or tongue. Husband or wife may do this to their partner. It is typically used as part of foreplay, but some couples will use it as the "main event" if intercourse isn't an option (such as after the birth of a baby). Others enjoy it as much or more than intercourse, and make it a regular part of their sexual relationship.

WHAT IS ANAL SEX?

Anal sex is sexual activity involving the penetration of the anus. Anal sex finds its most frequent use in homosexual relationships and can be extremely damaging to the bodies of those who practice it. (From my personal study and perspective, anal sex is not normal or safe for heterosexual couples, however, this is something every couple has to prayerfully consider and decide for themselves. Some couples may be able to practice it in good conscience, but it should never a decision spurred by porn).

WHAT IS MASTURBATION?

Masturbation is the manual stimulation of sexual organs in order to achieve climax/sexual pleasure. Locker room jargon for guys refers to this as "jerking off". We will discuss masturbation in detail later in this book, as it is highly addictive and often used in conjunction with erotica or porn.

Sometimes couples will incorporate masturbation into foreplay, or will masturbate for one another in instances where intercourse is not possible (e.g., soon after having a baby). This kind of masturbation is not singular but mutual, and thus does not cause the distance and sexual separation that masturbating alone can cause. Read more about this in chapter six.

CAN YOU HAVE SEX ON YOUR PERIOD?

The short answer to this is yes, but not all couples love the idea of it. Sex is messy no matter what – there are a lot of bodily fluids involved! Some people are okay with just laying a towel down and/or using a condom during the wife's period for easy clean up, but others are grossed out by the idea. Every couple needs to decide what works for them. There is an increased risk of a urinary tract infection (UTI) if you have sex on your period, though, so make sure to clean yourself up afterward (using the restroom after sex is a great way to prevent a UTI, whether or not you're menstruating).

CAN YOU HAVE SEX WHILE PREGNANT?

I used to wonder how husbands went nine months without having sex while their wives were pregnant – that's how uninformed I was! Sex during pregnancy is not only possible, it is recommended! It helps balance hormones, release endorphins, boost sexual creativity (body changes make the usual positions more difficult) and induce labor. The prostaglandins in semen can also prepare the cervix for labor, encouraging baby's arrival closer to the due date rather than weeks overdue. Of course, if you have medical complications that make sex unadvisable, listen to your doctor.

WHAT IS SEX LIKE AFTER HAVING A BABY?

Sex after baby – typically begun after a six-week postpartum recovery - will vary depending on what happened during birth. Women who've had C-sections, episiotomies (cutting the perineum – theskin between the vagina and anus - so the baby can emerge), or long, difficult labors may be more tender for a longer period of time. The first few times the wife will need plenty of foreplay (and possibly extra lubrication like KY gel) to "warm her up" for intercourse. Her husband will need to be sensitive to her recovery as well.

Personally, my husband and I found post-baby sex to be even better than it was before. This could be because it's less frequent and therefore more meaningful, or perhaps because practice makes perfect! Either way, after our daughter was born, sex did not hurt like I expected. However, this will depend on many different factors as stated above, as well as how mentally relaxed you are during the experience.

The key to good sex, whether pre- or post-baby, is in our minds. The more focused and relaxed a couple is during sex, the better it is. In my own marriage, we keep baby items out of the bedroom, do not co-sleep with our children, and sleep train from an early age – our bedroom is our haven, and we protect that time as a couple.

WHAT ABOUT BIRTH CONTROL?

There are many different options for birth control, from hormonal pills, patches, and implants to condoms, diaphragms, and spermicides. Some of these stop ovulation and implantation; others are blockade methods that stop sperm from potentially entering the cervix. A full discussion of birth control is contained in Appendix Two of this book.

HOW A FLAWED VIEW OF SEX DESTROYS JOY

Prior to her wedding, many brides are thrown a lingerie shower – a party where her friends give her negligees, corsets, and "goodies" for her honeymoon and wedding night. I've attended many of these parties and am always thrilled by the joy of them: a true celebration of God's design.

Unfortunately, there never fails to be one women there who can't enjoy the festivities. She is obviously uncomfortable and unable to see how sex can be both sacred and celebratory: a privilege for Christian married women, and something to look forward to as a single. I am deeply saddened that her perspective – or her pain – has caused her to see sex as an untouchable subject, when Christian women have more to celebrate about sex than *all other women in the world.*

But when you associate sex only with sin, it becomes something dark. It becomes something foreign. **It ceases to be celebratory.**

This doesn't happen by accident. The enemy of our souls is also the enemy of our sexuality. If he can twist our perspective of sex, he can tear down our marriages from the inside out. He can tear down our character, our minds, and our identities. When we accept his lie that sex is either irresistible or inherently evil, our lives follow the trajectory of that extreme. Both promiscuity and legalism begin with a *lie*.

But the truth is far different. The truth is that our sexuality is part of our *created design*. It is a vehicle of the gospel. It is as much a part of us as our minds and emotions, and like our minds and emotions, our sexuality can glorify God.

For the Christian woman, a lingerie shower is an opportunity to celebrate true sexual freedom. It is a chance to revel in the redemption of God over a sexuality that may have once been captive to sin. It is a chance to praise God for His protection over a sexuality prevented from pain. It is a chance to join hands with women – married and unmarried – and proclaim the glory of God through our femininity.

A Christian lingerie shower is a celebration of God's design.

For too long, we have separated our sexuality from the rest of our lives. We talk about the influence of Christ on our minds, our clothes, and our service – but we forget that His is a *holistic* influence. When we invite Jesus in, we invite His influence into *every* part of who we are. We allow Him to transform our understanding of ourselves.

We should invite Jesus to our lingerie showers because we *invite Jesus into our lives*. Our sexuality is as available to His transforming influence as our spending habits and our words. We don't take a break from Jesus to throw an awesome pre-marriage party. We invite Him into it. And in doing so, we invite accountability, unity, and honor into our sexuality and our relationships.

We need to allow the Bible to transform our understanding of sex; to see it the way God sees it and to celebrate that design. We need to take joy in our friends who boldly follow God's plan for their sexuality, celebrating their endurance and tenacity. We need to let go of self-consciousness and see the big picture: that sexuality doesn't begin when we say our wedding vows. It's part of who we are. **And if it's already part of who we are, it has a purpose to serve for God's kingdom.**

So let's become women of celebration, because the world needs more of us. The world needs more women who celebrate honor and stand up for redemptive sexuality.

The world needs more women to boldly share their testimonies so others can have hope.

The world needs more women to see the beauty of their own sexuality when used according to God's design, and to live out that freedom in front of their friends.

There are enough Christian women to meet this need, but it will remain unmet. It will remain unmet unless we allow God to remove the lies we've believed about sex and replace them with His truth – that in marriage,

...sex is not bad – *It is beautiful.*

...sex is not gross – *It is God-designed.*

...sex is not dirty – *It is holy.*

Sex is something to celebrate. The world doesn't hold rights to it. *We do.*

We – Christian women – are sexually *free*. Free from the pain of sin. Free to use our sexuality for a higher purpose – not be dictated by its demands.

So at your next lingerie shower, I hope you celebrate. I hope you laugh and tease and glorify God for the grace He's given us, because ours is a celebratory sexuality – unparalleled in this world.

This is by no means an exhaustive list of sexual topics, and for many of you it may have been a very basic overview of what you already know. For those who were not privileged with a "sex talk", however, I hope this chapter has broadened your understanding of sexuality and quelled some of the fears you may have harbored about sex.

QUESTIONS TO CONSIDER:

1. *Did your parents have "the talk" with you? Did you feel it gave you an accurate picture of sex?*

2. *Was any of this information new to you? If yes, how has it changed your view of sex?*

3. *How did you feel as you read this chapter? Identify any areas of fear you need to bring to the Lord.*

WHY GOD DESIGNED SEX FOR MARRIAGE

Whether out of fear, legalism, or just ignorance, many churches take one of two tacks when it comes to sex:

1) Ignore the topic completely,

2) Emphasize the evil of pre- or extramarital sex without ever discussing the nature of sex itself.

This leaves church-going girls with questions about both the nature *and* the details of sex, but afraid to ask because the stigma is so strong.

Outside the sanctuary, there is a different kind of world. Here sex is trumpeted as an achievement, a badge of honor, and a source of value. Told to both avoid sex and be "in the world but not of it", many Christian girls spend their days playing whack-a-mole with sexual topics, never truly *understanding* sex in their frantic effort to remain pure. Meanwhile, the world screams, "It's natural! It's good! It's wonderful! It makes you feel great and loved! Don't let religion control your choices!"

Our girls stand at a crossroads asking:

If God is good like I've been taught, and God made sex, why is sex bad?

Why does everyone else seem to think sex is great?

Is Christian sex the only kind that's bad?

These are sad but necessary questions, and they lead us to the world's primary argument for extramarital sex: "If it feels good, affirms me, and makes me feel loved (however temporarily), it cannot be wrong."

IF IT FEELS RIGHT, HOW COULD IT BE WRONG?

At first glance, "if it feels good, do it" makes sense. But the logic of this argument is fundamentally flawed. With this train of thought, we could justify anything.

If we determine moral issues based on individual feelings, there is no standard for right or wrong at all. The standard for good and evil has to come from something *outside* of mankind, or truth is nothing more than personal opinion. Just because something 'feels good' does not mean it is the right thing to do for ourselves or for others. This is especially true when it comes to sexuality.

Sex is not just a 'natural' bodily function. It involves thoughts and emotions that heighten the sexual experience and are inexplicably tied to our minds and hearts. Part of what makes sex so desirable is the sense of closeness we experience when we participate in it.

I was recently watching the movie *How to Lose a Guy in 10 Days* with my husband, Josh. One of the characters is known for frequent, week-long relationships, with break-ups shortly thereafter. This character typically slept with her dates within the first week. In one scene, she confesses that she sometimes cries or says, "I love you" after having sex. This emotional response to sex scared off the men she was dating, leaving her in the aftermath of another failed relationship.

The movie presents this girl as an emotional whack-job for acting this way. But in reality, those emotions are a natural and necessary part of sex! We are *supposed* to experience holistic intimacy. Sex was designed for emotional and physical closeness, not for one-night stands. If we followed the subliminal messages of *How to Lose a Guy*, we would stifle our emotions, separate sex from our desire for a lasting love, and continue to give ourselves to men who use us for physical pleasure alone.

In the Old Testament, sex is described with the verbs, "to know" (Gen. 4:1, 4:25, 21:2, 24:67). Marital sex is the most glorious example of the intimate relationship God desires with mankind. It is the kind of relationship founded on commitment, faithfulness, mutual love, and complete vulnerability. I love this verse from Proverbs that reveals the contrast between illicit sex and marital sex:

> *"Drink water from your own cistern, flowing water from your own well. Should your springs be*

scattered abroad, streams of water in the streets? Let them be for yourself alone, and not for strangers with you. Let your fountain be blessed, and rejoice in the wife of your youth, a lovely deer, a graceful doe. Let her breasts fill you at all times with delight; be intoxicated always in her love." (Prov. 5:15-19

Scattered, streets, strangers: This is the life of a sexual nomad. This is what happens when we refuse to commit to the beauty of God-designed love. Marital sex is a reservoir of satisfaction. It is not the 'scattered streams' of illicit sex. It is a place to rejoice, delight, and be completely intoxicated with love, not overcome with temporary lust. It is a place to feel the height of emotion, and if we are moved to tears and 'I love you', we need not be ashamed.

Yes, there will be times where the experience isn't "the best". Sex takes practice! But in a relationship founded on commitment, sex is a journey husband and wife walk together. In so doing, they are progressively sanctified as they give themselves with patience, gentleness, and real love – the kind that commits to never, ever leave.

As women, we long to be pursued, won over, and wanted by a man. This is a high and holy desire: one given and designed by God. When God tells us to reserve sex for marriage, He is not telling us to deny the existence of our desires or be ashamed that they exist. The Designer of sex has revealed to us the blueprint for a fulfilling sexual relationship.

But God's design for sex is based on *real* love. It is good to desire that kind of love. But when a desire for love is reduced to a desire for sex alone, we miss the point entirely. Sex feels awesome - but that isn't its purpose. The purpose of sex is unity (Mark 10:8), service of one another (1 Cor. 7:1-40) and pure, faithful love (Heb. 13:4). God's design for sex is motivated by love. The world's design is driven by lust.

WHAT IS LUST?

Lust is a sensual appetite which, when embraced and idolized, gives birth to sin. Even in the church lust has been watered down and accepted as an inevitable part of dating relationships and single sexuality. This should not be the case! But to defeat lust, we must first go to God's Word and see if He indicates that lust is, in His view, a sin.

- The lust of the flesh and of the eyes belongs to the world (1 John 2:16). We are NOT of the world (John 15:19).
- Lust limits our ability to fight against sin and pollutes our hearts (2 Tim. 2:4, 22). This should concern us, since the **pure** in heart will see God (Matt. 5:8).
- Lust wages war against our souls (1 Peter 2:11).
- Lustful minds conform us to the world (Romans 12:2).

If we are to fulfill God's will (which is for us to be holy: 1 Thess. 4:3-8), the fruits of lust cannot be found in our lives. Our biological urges are not lust; they become lustful when we elevate them above our call to "be holy as He is holy" (1 Pet. 1:15).

Why is lust wrong?

- **Lust objectifies**. Lust of any kind is a focused and almost obsessive attention on attaining something. It is not patient or willing to give up its rights. A lustful mind is more focused on its desire than on the consequences of that desire. It is irrational: Both sensual and insensitive.

- **Lust satisfies itself first.** Lust is focused on satisfying a *want* that it perceives as a *need*. If lust cannot receive what it wants, it might just take it by force.

- **Lust twists God's plan.** Lust takes God's plan for sex out of context. God's context for sex is marriage because covenant is required for intimacy. Lust focuses on the *feelings* of sex without the *meaning* of sex.

- **Lust usurps God's authority.** Choosing to lust after someone essentially says, "I am god of this area of my life: I will dictate the parameters, limits, and morality of my own sexuality." When we choose lust our greatest transgression is not the action itself but our rebellion against God. Lust is pride: an attempt to step above His standard of holiness. This is the same thing Satan did before He was cast out of heaven (Ezek. 28:12-15).

HOW CAN LOVE BE A SIN?

"I'm in a loving relationship. We love each other, so I have a hard time believing God would have a problem with us having sex."

This common objection from the world has also been adopted

by Christian women and men. But this objection has a fatal flaw: *The definition of love.*

God has requires marriage for sex because love is founded on **sacrifice** and **commitment.** To understand love as God defines it (and as He expects us to love others), we need to look at how He loves us:

> *"Your love, O LORD, reaches to the heavens, your faithfulness to the skies. Your righteousness is like the mighty mountains, your justice like the great deep. O LORD, you preserve both man and beast. How priceless is your unfailing love! Both high and low among men find refuge in the shadow of your wings." (Psalm 36:5-7)*

> *"Can a mother forget her nursing child? Can she feel no love for the child she has borne? But even if that were possible, I would not forget you! See, I have written your name on the palms of my hands." (Is. 49:15-16)*

> *"The LORD appeared to us in the past, saying: I have loved you with an everlasting love; I have drawn you with loving-kindness." (Jer. 31:3)*

God's love is everlasting. It is faithful. And most of all, it is sacrificial. God sent Jesus to purify us so that we could have a holy relationship with Him.

God's love is always meant to make us holy. The world's "love" can temporarily satisfy, but it can never bridge the gap between us and God. Sex outside of marriage separates us from perfect relationship with Him. We cannot have a thriving relationship with Jesus Christ and simultaneously be committing extramarital sexual sin. A true, devoted follower of Christ will make every effort to uphold the holiness of God:

> *"Therefore, since Christ suffered in the flesh, arm yourselves also with the same resolve... in order to live the remaining time in the flesh, no longer for human desires but for God's will." (1 Peter 4:1-2)*

For those who align their hearts and lives with His love, God is ready to take them back with open arms. There is still hope. There is always redemption.

WHAT ABOUT DIVORCE?

God's original plan for marriage NEVER included divorce. Divorce is a product of sin in this world: Whether by unfaithfulness, abuse, neglect, or pure selfishness. Jesus was very straightforward about this in Mark 10:2-10:

> *"Some Pharisees came and tested him by asking, "Is it lawful for a man to divorce his wife?" "What did Moses command you?" he replied. They said, "Moses permitted a man to write a certificate of divorce and send her away." "It was because your hearts were hard that Moses wrote you this law," Jesus replied. "But at the beginning of creation God 'made them male and female.' 'For this reason a man will leave his father and mother and be united to his wife, and the two will become one flesh.' So*

they are no longer two, but one. Therefore, what God has joined together, let man not separate."

Divorce is a product of our culture, not a product of God's marital design. He does not want his children to be hurt, grieved, and divided by divorce, but sin's influence has made broken marriages a fixture in our society. Even so, God's standards are not altered by cultural trends. God will still protect sex behind the bond of marriage because *intimacy requires covenant*. God values marriage and sex - regardless of how little value our culture grants them.

This said, saving sex for marriage – on its own - does not prevent divorce. God never indicated that it would. *Being a virgin does not prevent divorce.*

Our marriages are as safe from divorce as they are close to Christ. This is why we cannot battle lust with legalism, or protect purity with a bunch of rules! We are called to be pure out of a love for God, and it is this same love for God that prevents divorce. It takes the same selflessness to save sex for marriage as it does to make marriage work. **Virginity doesn't guarantee good marriage: love for God does.**

SEX IS NOT "BAD"

Sex in and of itself is not 'bad': it is one of the crowning glories of God's creation. Eve was brought to Adam at the conclusion of God's creative work in Genesis 1-2. Sex was designed to be enjoyed. And – as previously discussed – God's only requirement for sexual fulfillment is that we *be married*.

Our sexuality has a grand purpose: It is a means for us to glorify God! The question then becomes "Do I honor Christ with my sexuality the same way I honor Him with my career decisions, thoughts, and words?"

Our desire for sex is a testament to God's grace. We shouldn't stuff it away and pretend it doesn't exist. Neither should we prance around the church parking lot advertising our virginity. And we should never allow Satan to hold us captive with past sexual failures. No: We allow our sexual desires to be the good and wonderful thing God designed them to be, neither worshiping them nor ignoring their existence.

Paula Rinehart says in her book *Sex and the Soul of a Woman*:

> *"The second path [holding on to hope] is harder... But it leads to a place worth going, and this makes all the difference. To live in the rarer air of the in-between – neither shutting down desire nor demanding it be fulfilled in a particular way – is your own heart's journey in what is means to trust God with your life."*

We have to trust God when it comes to our sexuality. We have to trust that His plan for sex really is in our best interest. This kind of trust only comes from understanding who God is and just how much He truly loves us, His women.

QUESTIONS TO CONSIDER:

1. *How has the definition of lust changed your understanding of sexual sin?*

2. *How has the definition of love changed your understanding of purity?*

3. *Do you see how important God's love is to our understanding of sexuality? How will this impact your daily life?*

WHAT IF I'M NOT A VIRGIN?

The purity movement accomplished much good, but deep within its underpinnings lies an unanswered question: *Will God still love me if I am not a virgin?*

In an effort to prevent sexual sin, purity culture lost its ability to restore the broken. And though the movement sought to teach us God's design for sex, it failed to extend God's hope to the hurting. But here is the difficult truth: Purity is not about virginity.

Purity is not about virginity because virginity – in and of itself - is *not God's goal.*

Let me be clear: The Bible states that God's design for sex is marriage (discussed in the preceding chapter). Pre-marital and extra-marital sex, as well as acts of foreplay prior to marriage, are outside His will. But purity is *more* than abstinence, just as modesty is more than putting on clothes. Purity is a posture of the heart which keeps us in relationship with God.

TRUE PURITY RESTORES HOPE

Love for God is the only motive to purity that will stand the test of time. And because the purpose of purity is to keep us in relationship with God, virginity itself *cannot* be God's goal. In Christ, purity is available to all – even those who have sinned sexually. If virginity were God's goal, would there be hope for victims of rape? Would there be redemption for those who have failed? Would there be forgiveness for those who have sinned?

There would not.

Our Lord's arms were stretched open on the Cross to bring back the wounded. This speaks to God's mission: Holiness - not just virginity - is His goal.

This does not grant us a free pass to sexually indulge. As Paul says, "What shall we say then? Are we to continue in sin so that grace may increase? May it never be! How shall we who died to sin still live in it?" (Romans 6:1-2) God's gift of holiness (through Jesus) removes condemnation and frees us to live a righteous lifestyle. This in turn enables us to have perfect communion with an all-holy God – something we cannot have apart from Christ. When we accept Christ's sacrifice, we are made holy by a loving, restorative God – regardless of whether or not virginity is intact.

God's heart is neither condemnation (Rom. 8:1) nor separation (2 Pet. 3:9). He has a holy standard because only holy people can know Him. Through Jesus, He made us holy for the sake of His love. This is our only chance at relationship with a perfect God.

You might be thinking, "Okay Phylicia, I sort of get it. But everywhere I look Christian women seem to be perfectly pure. I've messed up. I don't know anyone who has been restored, only those who have always been pure." My friend, you are not alone. Restoration is a theme throughout all of Scripture, especially evident in the lives of women. Let's look at a few.

RUTH (RUTH 1-4)

Ruth was married to the son of Naomi for ten years (Ruth 1:4-5) before meeting Boaz (Ruth 2:4-5). If you haven't read this little book, I recommend starting it as your quiet time this week. Ruth's story is all about restoration!

Ruth was married once before she met Boaz. She was most definitely not a virgin, and more than that, she was a foreigner. Yet despite her heritage and history she became the great-grandmother of King David. Ruth was part of the family line that eventually led to Jesus Himself!

If virginity were God's goal, Ruth could not have found love again after the death of her husband. Because Ruth sought God and aligned her actions with worship of Him, she became a pivotal part of His redemption plan.

THE WOMAN AT THE WELL (JOHN 4:1-45)

The woman at the well is a case study in failed relationships. Jesus pointed out that she had had five husbands and the man she lived with at the time was not her husband at all (John 4:17-18).

Jesus saw this woman as more than a body; she was also a soul. While Jesus *acknowledged* her past, He looked beyond it to her future. Jesus was so intentional toward this woman he waited at the well at noon – long after the typical time women came to draw water. He was also in Samaria, a place no 'godly' rabbi would dare to tread. Jesus drew out this woman's story as she drew water from the well and offered her hope for new life – new purity. And just as He accepted water from her hand, she accepted redemption from His.

THE ADULTERESS (JOHN 8:1-11)

During the Feast of Tabernacles (or Booths), the Pharisees brought before Jesus a woman caught in adultery (John 8:4-5). According to Mosaic Law she was worthy to be stoned, condemned by her transgression. But because Jesus is the Messiah, He has authority over the Law and paid the penalty for ALL sin. He would take her stoning – and He could and did forgive her.

"Woman, where are they? Does no one condemn you?" He asked.

And she answered: "No one, Lord." (John 8:11)

Had she sinned? Definitely. But the Law that condemned points us to the Hope of restoration: Jesus Christ. When Jesus stood up to the Pharisees He did not deny that the adulteress had sinned – but He revealed His authority *over* condemnation.

Jesus is the intercessor between our failings and God's holiness. It is in Jesus that we stand restored, lifted from the mud to "Go, and sin no more." (John 8:11)

THE SINFUL WOMAN (LUKE 7:36-50)

She rushed into the room, disheveled, weeping and clutching a flask. She had spent all her money, everything she had earned. Dirty money, earned with her body. She didn't care about how they looked at her anymore – because in His eyes she saw love. It was the kind of love that no longer saw her as untouchable. It was the kind of love that gave her hope.

Luke 7 depicts the 'sinful woman' who enters the Pharisee's house to wash Jesus' feet. Jesus' host neither washed the feet of his guests nor provided someone to do so – perhaps more concerned with the pomp of hosting a celebrity than actually serving his guest. But when the woman entered, she had nothing to prove except her gratitude for grace. She poured out all she had as an offering on Jesus' feet.

If virginity were God's goal, Jesus could have joined his Pharisaical host in thinking, "[I know]...who and what sort of woman this is who is touching [me], for she is a sinner." (Luke 7:39) But Jesus did not turn her away. Instead, He extended hope: "Therefore I tell you, her sins, which are many, are forgiven—for she loved much. But he who is forgiven little, loves little." And he said to her, "Your sins are forgiven." (Luke 7:47-48)

MARY MAGDALENE
(LUKE 24:10, MATT. 28:1, MARK 16:1,9)

Mary Magdalene was one of the first people to see Jesus after His resurrection. While there is no evidence that she is the sinful woman in Luke 7, Mary was possessed by seven demons. She also hailed from the city of Magdala, a town three miles from Capernaum known for its harlotry. Whether or not Mary was a virgin we do know that she was racked with oppression by these seven spirits before Jesus freed her from that bondage.

Like Mary, we too can be oppressed. We may be oppressed by cultural influence, public opinion, inadequacy, doubt, and lust. But also like Mary, freedom from bondage is available through Jesus Christ.

In Luke 13:10-17 we meet a woman disabled by a spirit, unable to 'fully straighten herself'. This woman was destined to continue through life a cripple, never able to fully embrace the freedom of walking and running... until Jesus.

> *"When Jesus saw her, he called her over and said to her, "Woman, you are freed from your disability." And he laid his hands on her, and immediately she was made straight, and she glorified God." (Luke 13:12-13)*

But there were some who would rather the woman remain a cripple than see their traditions altered. Jesus had no tolerance for this hypocrisy:

> *"Then the Lord answered him, "You hypocrites! Does not each of you on the Sabbath untie his ox or his donkey from the manger and lead it away to water it? And ought not this woman, a daughter of Abraham whom Satan bound for eighteen years, be loosed from this bond on the Sabbath day?" As he said these things, all his adversaries were put to shame, and all the people rejoiced at all the glorious things that were done by him.' (Luke 13:16-17)*

Our God doesn't want us walking through life as sexual cripples. Maybe you have failed. Maybe you have lost your virginity. These *are* contrary to God's plan for sex, but our God reaches to you in your crippled state, saying: "Ought not this woman, a daughter of mine whom Satan has bound for years, be loosed from this bond TODAY?" (Luke 13:16)

We place a high value on virginity because God created us with a need for intimacy and that intimacy is designed for oneness. **But if God's goal were virginity, there would be no hope for millions of women around the globe.** When the church presents virginity as a prize to be won, it has missed God's goal and elevated legalism above the mission of Christ.

God's goal is not virginity. **His heart is holiness.**

In Jesus, you have restoration no matter what your history. In Jesus, you are a new woman: a new kind of virgin walking in freedom to please God. You are a "priestess queen" (1 Peter 2), a woman of strength, dignity, and holiness because that is who Christ made you – regardless of who you were before.

QUESTIONS TO CONSIDER:

1. *In what ways do you identify with the stories of the women in this chapter?*

2. *How does setting your eyes on holiness – not just virginity – give you hope?*

3. *Does this view of redemptive sexuality change your view of God's character?*

HOW TO LIVE AS
A FORGIVEN WOMAN

How could God forgive me of something I've done again and again?

If you've asked this question, you're not alone. It's a pressing concern for many believers. Our renewed spirit longs to restore relationship but that hope is limited by doubt. Will God *really* forgive? And what does forgiveness look like?

Sin is sin. Whether gossip, lying, pride or extramarital sex, all sin is breaking the law of God (1 John 3:4) Sin is offensive to God because God is holy and perfect (Is. 6:1-5). Because man chose sin at the beginning (Genesis 3) all of us are born with a natural tendency to offend God (Romans 5:12).

Unlike other sins, sexual sin affects the body, emotions, mind, *and* spirit (1 Cor. 6:18). Sex was designed to be a thrilling experience in marriage, in which context the physical-emotional-spiritual connection is intense and fulfilling. But when removed from that context, sex has the power to twist our self-perception, spiral us into deeper sin, and most of all separate us spiritually from God.

So what do we do if we have transgressed God's law, offended God, and separated ourselves from a peaceful relationship with Him? Is there hope for those enduring the consequences of sexual sin?

YES! There is hope! Embracing forgiveness is not easy: We battle guilt, shame, and doubt. But in Christ, we all have the opportunity to walk as conquerors in the grace of God. The following steps will help you begin this journey.

ACKNOWLEDGE THAT GOD SEES ILLICIT SEX AS SIN

Though Jesus forgave the prostitute (Luke 7) and the adulteress (John 8), He didn't pretend their actions were acceptable. The very act of forgiveness literally means to *cancel a debt to holiness.* Their actions were sinful, or there would be nothing to forgive! Secondly, Jesus drew on the most powerful motive to obedience: Love.

The first step to forgiveness and restoration is to acknowledge sin. It is not enough to be "sorry" we got caught, afraid our parents will find out, or scared the church will think differently of us – that's not repentance. Repentance is a change of heart.

REPENT TO THE LORD

Let's clear something up right away: Repentance does not mean you will never sin again. Repentance is a change of heart, not just behavior, and focusing on behavior reform (or behavior failure) misses the point. Our behavior is only a symptom of what's going on inside our hearts. Genuine repentance starts with recognition of how sin affects God, and what it takes for God to forgive it.

Neither is repentance remorse. Feeling "bad" over our sin is not the same as a repentant heart. Repenting is a complete 180 degree turn from what was done to the life God offers through Christ – a turn that often requires sacrifice.

Repentance is not merely behavior reform! Neither is it something we do in a one-time salvation decision. Confession of sin – and turning from it - is our demonstration of faith beyond salvation, into the everyday relationship with God. If we say we are one with Jesus we can't hold onto Him with one hand and sin with the other (1 John 1:6-7).

What if I genuinely repent of the sin, but when the temptation arises again, I fail?

When we truly repent, we will make every effort to remove sin from our lives. However, God gives grace for the growing process. Do you recall what he told Peter about forgiveness?

> *"Then Peter came and said to Him, "Lord, how often shall my brother sin against me and I forgive him? Up to seven times?" Jesus said to him, "I do not say to you, up to seven times, but up to seventy times seven." (Matt. 18:21-22)*

If God commands us to forgive over and over and over again, how much more patient is He with us and our weaknesses? I hope this gives you a glimpse of how loving and kind is our God! God's kindness draws us to repentance, and His mercy keeps us there.

> "...do you think lightly of the riches of His kindness and tolerance and patience, not knowing that the kindness of God leads you to repentance?" (Romans 2:4)

This change of mind leads to a change of behavior. We must align our lives with repentance to see the fruit in our lives. We are only as safe from sin as we are close to Christ!

ACCEPT HIS GRACE DAILY

Grace is NOT getting what we deserve; it is mercy extended to us rather than judgment. The consequence of sin is separation from God – which God defines as both spiritual and eternal death (Rom. 6:23). Paul clearly articulates this in Romans chapter six:

> "But now that you have been set free from sin and have become slaves of God, the fruit you get leads to sanctification and its end, eternal life. For the wages of sin is death, but the free gift of God is eternal life in Christ Jesus our Lord." (Rom. 6:22-23)

Did you read that first verse? Now you have been SET FREE from sin! The fruit of repentance leads to:

- Present-day sanctification, and
- The end result: eternal life with God after death.

God's definition of 'eternal life' is 'abundant life'. It doesn't just indicate quantity of life, but quality of life! Because God loves you, He wants to bless you and see you live the abundant-quality life He created you to experience.

> *"I am the door; if anyone enters through Me, he will be saved, and will go in and out and find pasture. The thief comes only to steal and kill and destroy; I came that they may have life, and have it abundantly." (John 10:9-10)*

So you've accepted your sin, you've repented of the sin, and you acknowledge God's forgiveness: now you need to walk in that forgiveness daily. You must pray for the strength to believe it and receive it. You must cling to it, hope in it, and trust it. And you must trust the Giver of Grace, who loves you and extends forgiveness for the very reason of keeping His relationship with you, the apple of His eye!

Satan, on the other hand, wants us to live in condemnation. When we allow him to resurrect past sins, we give him power over our identity-perception. We cease to see ourselves as forgiven and instead see ourselves as failures. When this pattern is propagated, it leads to despair and ultimately repetition of former sins.

Do not listen to those lies! If you have repented to Christ, THERE IS NO CONDEMNATION :

> *"Therefore there is now no condemnation for those who are in Christ Jesus. For the law of the*

Spirit of life in Christ Jesus has set you free from the law of sin and of death..." (Romans 8:1-2)

Choose daily to accept your new identity. Revel in it. Live in it. God expects it of you! One of my favorite verses is 1 Peter 2:9-10, which illustrates this identity that is YOURS and MINE in Christ Jesus:

"But you are A CHOSEN RACE, A royal PRIESTHOOD, A HOLY NATION, A PEOPLE FOR God's OWN POSSESSION, so that you may proclaim the excellencies of Him who has called you out of darkness into His marvelous light; for you once were NOT A PEOPLE, but now you are THE PEOPLE OF GOD; you had NOT RECEIVED MERCY, but now you have RECEIVED MERCY...." (1 Pet. 2:9-10)

My friend, here is how God sees you:

- Chosen
- Royal
- Priestess
- Holy
- His
- Pure
- Wanted
- Under Grace

All you have to do is believe Him.

SET UP SAFEGUARDS

Repentance does not guarantee obedience. We have to choose to align our lives with the heart-choice of repentance. This is where standards come into play.

Legalism puts the rules at the front end of this conversation. Some women are told to be pure as a bargaining chip for God's love and salvation. For them, purity is driven by fear of judgment and wrath. This is backwards theology, and it is not the gospel.

God *does* hate impurity because He is pure. But God also knows that love is the motivator to obedience. When God gave Adam and Eve 'rules' in the Garden of Eden, obedience was inspired by love for God and a desire to maintain relationship with Him. When they held that relationship in high esteem, breaking standards didn't occur. But the moment Eve entertained the question, "Did God really say...?", she was herself asking, "Is God really worthy to be trusted?"

And the moment she ceased to trust God, she broke His standards.

In the same way, we must guard against temptation; we must acknowledge our weaknesses and place hedges to ensure strength.

Standards aren't the point, but they are a reflection of our dedication. Purity doesn't just happen, especially for those of us weak in this area. You must be on guard. You are a target of Satan who knows your weak points. Be aware, and be dedicated, and above all, stay close to Christ.

LIVE ACCORDING TO YOUR IDENTITY

Remember what Peter said about your identity in Christ? You are chosen, royal, holy, pure, and wanted. You are no longer captive to sin! You are holy and righteous in God's eyes. If you fall again – RUN back to Christ! Satan would love to keep you hiding in the bushes stitching fig leaves. But God is the Father, running down the road to you, His wayward child, arms open to receive you (Luke 15:11-32).

With love like this, why would we ever want to take advantage of His grace? When Mary Magdalene the prostitute wept on Jesus' feet in a room of condescending men, she was more conscious of her sin than many of us will ever be. But that consciousness of sin brought even greater consciousness of grace, which Jesus explained when He said: "Therefore, I tell you, her many sins have been forgiven–as her great love has shown. But whoever has been forgiven little loves little." (Luke 7:47)

Separation from God by sin makes His grace so much sweeter. The fact that God is not only able but willing to make us pure in His eyes is the very core of the gospel message! I think a personal testimony illustrates this best, so I asked my husband, Josh, to share his story of redemptive purity:

> *"Although I was raised in a Christian home, as soon as I was old enough to pursue relationships with girls, I broke loose. The result of this was that*

many girls were dishonored by me, and eventually I lost my virginity. When I first entered a relationship with my wife, Phylicia, I couldn't tell her that I had remained abstinent for her. Losing my virginity before marriage made me realize the pain of extramarital sex, which did help me refrain from repeating this sin in my relationship with Phylicia.

If I had a do-over, I would have refrained from it the first time and avoided that guilt altogether. I wish that I could have told my wife that she was my 'First'. But the reason I was able to have a wonderful, guilt-free, wedding night with my wife is because I knew that it was our first time with one another. I know that I have been redeemed by God's grace, which I sought daily during our dating relationship. It was, and still is, only by God's grace that my wife and I are able to be free of our guilt and shame of the past. It is His redeeming grace that makes our love pure."

God gives us grace for today, grace for tomorrow, grace in the moment, and grace for eternity. We don't deserve it. We never can. The point is not US deserving it but GOD loving us enough to see past our unworthiness. We should be overwhelmed with His goodness, so thankful for His grace!

When I failed God sexually, I asked Him: *Can I ever be who I was before?*

God never answered that prayer. He never made me who I

was before. Who I was before thought pure hearts and bodies were math equations to get good things out of life.

God didn't make me and my husband who we were before: He made us new. We are completely redeemed, restored versions of our former selves. He can and will do the same for you.

HOW DO I ACCEPT GRACE?

There is a difference between knowing truth and truly embracing it with all that we have. When we fail God, Satan sweeps in with guilt and despair to keep us from His restoration. If he can convince us not to accept God's grace, he can lead us into a pattern of repeated sin.

Sometimes we accept *partial* grace. It's easier to accept a half-forgiveness: we're okay with a forgiveness 'stamped across the sin', but we can't believe the sin is wiped away. Can our hasty words, rash temper, arrogance, selfishness, and blundered relationships could be so forgiven they aren't even there anymore?

But if we only believe *partial grace* we only receive *partial joy.*

Our experiences try to overshadow the strength and power of God. The more we focus on our life experience, the smaller God seems. But if Jesus is not King over our experience, He isn't a king to us at all.

All of life is an experience: relationships with parents, hurtful words by friends, annoying jobs, sexual abuse, sinful choices – these are a part of existence in a fallen world. If we, as Christians, believe that these experiences are too great for God to overcome, we have effectively dethroned the King of Kings in our hearts. We exist Christian in name; atheist in living.

Don't think I'm demeaning our experiences or saying we should 'just get over it'. I have experiences of my own that threaten to drown out my view of God. But that's the problem: I've tended those wounds, bandaged them, stressed over them, even begged God to heal them, but never quite believed He would. I believed That somehow I was responsible for part of my healing: an emotional self-flagellation that made me feel even more inadequate.

The scandal of grace is this: we don't deserve the gift, but it's still a gift. We can take it, or we can leave it unopened and live in bondage the rest of our lives. Jesus is the 'ultimate gift to mankind'. But what does this even mean for us today?

The gift of grace is realized in our lives to the degree it is accepted. It feels wrong to accept grace. We get scared we'll be one of those who 'sins more that grace may abound' (Rom. 6:1). But here's the thing: when you acknowledge that God became man for the express purpose of giving grace to sinners like you and me, it becomes much easier to accept the gift. And when you accept it, the last thing you want to do is sin against the Giver.

It may feel safe to take a 'measure' of grace: just enough to make us feel confessed but not enough to be indebted.

Just enough to acknowledge our sin, but not enough to free us from our past.

Just enough to get it off our chest, but not enough to get it out of our hearts.

So we live joyless and un-triumphant, never allowing the King to fully reign in our hearts – never knowing what Jesus meant when He said, "Fear not, for I have overcome!" (John 16:33)

Jesus' birth was the birth of a King: not a king of earthly nations or military force, but a King of righteous and holy hearts. His power was not used just to humble world leaders but to completely cleanse the dirty, wholly heal the broken, and forever secure a place for us.

God took great measures to bring grace to earth that day. Will we accept it?

We don't want to accept the gift of grace because we realize just how much we don't deserve it.

But that's the point.

Do you know why the woman in Luke 7 was confident to approach Jesus, perfume in hand, pouring out her tears and her living on His feet? *She believed and accepted His grace.* If she let her past sins and insecurities wield power over her heart, she never would have dared set foot in that room. But the grace of God was her confidence, just as 1 John 5:14 says:

> *"This is the confidence we have in approaching God: that if we ask anything according to his will, he hears us.."*

And Jesus heard the cry of her heart, saying:

> *"I tell you – her sins, which are many, are forgiven her."* (Luke 7:47).

Hebrews 4:16 says:

> *"Let us then approach God's throne of grace with confidence, so that we may receive mercy and find grace to help us in our time of need."*

We can approach the throne of our King with confidence in His grace. He knows our weaknesses (Heb. 4:15); He knows we will fail Him. But each time we approach His throne to confess our failings, to bring Him our burdens, and relinquish the past, we renew the relationship He died to ensure. Sin pains Him, but "there is rejoicing in the presence of the angels of God over one sinner who repents." (Luke 15:10).

We often think faith is a one-stop shop used for salvation, after which we pull ourselves up by the bootstraps and 'go it alone' – what some call 'practical atheism'. But every day of our lives, every burden of our past, and every struggle of today is part of a series of faith decisions: conscious choices to believe God is present and powerful. We can choose to live faithless, Christian in name only; or we can accept grace, believe God, and truly walk by faith and not by sight.

So don't cringe from grace, dear girl. Don't cower from the love of God, refusing to open the gift He has given you. The central message of the gospel is the GOOD NEWS of grace to the undeserving, hope to the hopeless, and a future for those of every past.

QUESTIONS TO CONSIDER:

1. *Do you notice a cycle of sin in your life? This can be anything – not just sexual sin.*

2. *Have you repented of this sin? Remember: it is not presumptuous to come to God shortly after sinning! He is your only hope for redemption – don't wait to come to Him!*

3. *Do you struggle to accept grace? Begin implementing the thoughts and affirmations of this chapter. Focus on who Christ is and what He has done – not on who you are and what you are not. Grace is a gift!*

WHY GETTING MARRIED WON'T STOP SEXUAL SIN

For the Christian girl struggling with lust, no day is an easy one. What most perceive as a "man's problem" is largely a woman's problem, too, and it's easy to see marriage as the solution to this struggle.

We've let this mentality thrive. We've celebrated marriage as the haven for God-defined sexuality that it is, but we've forgotten something. We've forgotten that marriage can't fix a lust problem.

Satan targets sexuality because it is one of the most influential aspects of the human being. Because God designed sex for spiritual, emotional, and physical intimacy, it has incredible value. To protect this value, God requires a covenant of marriage in order to participate in sex.

Lust is simply a form of idolatry; worshiping desire instead of worshiping God. Because of the culture in which we live, the desire for sex is a subject of confusion and tension for Christian women. The world tells us to embrace the desire; the church tells us to ignore it. Left in a sexual-spiritual limbo, many girls resort to hiding their struggle, endlessly repeating the patterns of secret sin. In the throes of such a struggle, marital sex looks like the light at the end of the tunnel – but it's not.

Lust is not a sex problem, and it won't go away once you can have God-ordained sex. Lust is a *sin* problem. As such, lust is a spiritual issue only resolved with a spiritual solution.

Sexual desire is not the root of lust. Sex is simply the vehicle used to shift our focus away from God. The enemy uses sex to convince us God cannot satisfy, a belief that doesn't go away when we say "I do". By recognizing that lust is a spiritual battle – not a physical one – we can begin to fight lust *spiritually first*. And instead of burdening a spouse with the responsibility of "fixing" a problem they could never repair, we enter marriage equipped by God to overcome sinful desires.

Lust is inherently selfish. Marriage is selfless. These two are at odds with one another. The intimacy of marriage exposes sin, and the presence of another person makes lust that much more hurtful and burdensome in the life of the believer. The opportunity to have God-blessed sex won't remove the selfish, spiritual root of lust. If anything, it will exacerbate the problem. That's why we need to be intentional about this battle before *and* after marriage.

No couple will be perfectly selfless, and this covenant is not designed to solve our spiritual problems. Expecting marriage to redeem and restore is a set up for disillusionment. Rather than look to marriage as the solution for a struggle with lust, we should look to Christ. Christ Himself is the Redeemer and Restorer in both singleness and matrimony. This in mind, we can address lust at its root, daily walking in the Spirit to destroy selfishness and sin. This active faith allows us to live powerfully in the present and prepares us to enter marriage spiritually equipped for selfless love.

SEXUAL FREEDOM ONLY EXISTS WITH CHRIST

We already know that if lust were a sex problem, having sex would fix it - but it doesn't. Problems with porn, masturbation, fantasy and extramarital sex don't go away after the vows. In order to find freedom from sexual sin, we must go to the *source* of sexual freedom.

Our culture defines sexual freedom as having sex with whoever you want, when you want, where you want, as any gender you want. This is indeed a form of freedom, but it's a freedom with consequences.

The sexual freedom God offers is different. It is not freedom *to* but freedom *from*: He offers a sex life free from emotional, physical, and spiritual pain. He offers redemption for those who have transgressed His design. He offers purity to the impure. He offers great sex to those who recognize and embrace Him for their sexuality.

Because God takes vows very seriously – evidenced by His own blood covenants in Scripture – it's not enough to simply say, "We love one another." Vows must be made. A covenant must be cut. The boundaries of covenantal love protect true sexual freedom from being abused; covenant and intimacy are inseparable. The best sex is the result of intimacy in every sense: physical, emotional, and spiritual. It's one of the reasons Paul warned against being unequally yoked with unbelievers (2 Cor. 6:14). A marriage united in spirit leads to a sexual freedom unparalleled in this world.

This freedom can't be grasped with hands still clinging to sin. To celebrate our God-designed sexuality, we must let go of the lies. We must let go of the lust. Problems with sin are only conquered by the One who overcame it. Sexual freedom only exists with Christ.

The woman who embraces sexuality as the good and beautiful finds freedom to be her truest self. She finds *wholeness.*

The woman who pulls marriage off its pedestal and stands in faith on her blood-won freedom can laugh at the future. She finds *confidence.*

The woman who drops the crutch of lust she's been using as a coping mechanism finds her hands free to grasp abundant life.

She finds *Jesus.*

Marriage won't fix a lust problem because marriage is no savior. Fortunately for us, Jesus is.

CONQUERING A STRUGGLE WITH MASTURBATION

If you're a girl who struggles with masturbation, you probably think you're the only one in the world who does. You probably feel lonely, dirty, and hypocritical. You may be surprised to know you are *not* alone. Thousands of girls struggle in secret. I was on of them.

Biologically, masturbation is simply a body's response to stimulus. But because it involves our sexual design – which was meant for union in marriage – it's connected to our minds, emotions, and spirits. This is why masturbation often requires porn, erotica, or mental fantasy to "work".

Masturbation is addictive and focuses our minds on the flesh rather than the spirit (Gal. 5:16-18). As a woman continues to indulge fantasies or images contributing to this habit, she further strengthens the flesh over the spirit. Worse, this habit trains our minds into lust. Even if you are not currently in a relationship or have never dated, if you continue to feed your mind on the flesh it will be that much easier to give into physical desires once you ARE in a dating relationship (Col. 3:1-3).

As discussed earlier, getting married does not 'solve' masturbation. Women often turn to masturbation in marriage when their husbands do not satisfy them, which causes a dangerous breach of intimacy when this becomes a frequent practice. The open door caused by masturbation leads men *and* women into divided, not unified marriages (1 Cor. 16:13; 1 Cor. 10:12).

Masturbation, then, is an issue of the mind rather than the body. Viewed from a strictly biological perspective, it's easy to write this off as a physical exercise. But why then do God's daughters feel so guilty?

I believe we feel guilt because masturbation misses God's design for sex. Sex was designed to reflect God's intimacy with us: a peaceful, perfect union where we are loved in spite of our vulnerabilities and flaws. By nature, masturbation can never achieve intimacy because it is a solitary activity. In addition, it trains our minds to lust after images and scenarios God has not seen fit to give us, which is a form of covetousness and idolatry.

In Matthew 5:29-30, Jesus talked about temptation in a verse often applied to masturbation:

> *"If your right eye makes you stumble, tear it out and throw it from you; for it is better for you to lose one of the parts of your body, than for your whole body to be thrown into hell. If your right hand makes you stumble, cut it off and throw it from you; for it is better for you to lose one of the parts of your body, than for your whole body to go into hell."* (Matt. 5:29-30)

I don't believe Jesus was talking strictly about masturbation here, though He just finished speaking about the lust in the previous verse. Rather, Jesus is illustrating just how *harshly* we are to deal with sin in our lives. We are *to cut it off* and *gouge it out*. If something separates you from peace with God, do what it takes to get it out of your life.

WHAT DO I DO WITH THESE DESIRES?

If you've read this far, you're probably wondering "What are my options?!" How do we deal with sexual desire before marriage?

There are two kinds of desire: godly desire and sinful desire. Within our created bodies, God gives us an innate desire for companionship, love, and unity – all of which reflect of His character. Sex is also designed by God, which is why He is the one who determines where and when it is to be used. But just as our God-designed bodies get sick, grow old and die, so our desires can be twisted by this fallen world.

God gives us the capacity for desire; we choose what we do with it. Our sinful natures wrestle against God's design and we join the Apostle Paul in saying: "Wretched man that I am! Who will rescue me from this body of death?" (Rom. 7:24)

But as Paul says in Romans 7:25, we have a hope! Our rescuer is Jesus Christ. As our spiritual savior, He is automatically our sexual savior. He alone can help us honor Him with our desires.

Honoring God with our desires is a process, and it starts by acknowledging the source of temptation. God Himself tempts no one (James 1:13): In fact, James describes exactly where temptation comes from in the successive verses:

> *"...each person is tempted when he is drawn away and enticed by his own evil desires. Then after desire has conceived, it gives birth to sin, and when sin is fully grown, it gives birth to death." (James 1:14-15)*

Godly desires for companionship, love, and sex quickly become idols if we do not guard our hearts and minds (which we'll talk about in a moment). When we let our desires take precedent over Christ, formerly good things become the source of envy, covetousness, and lust.

There is a way to prevent this pattern of spiritual decline. The first step is to walk in the spirit.

When I was single, I felt like this "walking by the Spirit" thing was one big trick. It felt impossible. I resented God for making it so difficult to reject my sinful nature and do whatever this walking-by-the-Spirit thing was supposed to be. My desires were overwhelming. I spent most of my time playing spiritual whack-a-mole to keep them at bay. It was far from the free, confident Christian life God wanted for me.

The defeated life is never God's intention, but I was completely unaware of how I was defeating *myself*. I spent huge amounts of time thinking about marriage, relationships, or sex, and when I wasn't thinking about that I was thinking about ways to combat my desires. I was constantly on the defensive against my emotions. I thought my desires were just uncontrollable, but in reality my desires were controlling *me*.

When God calls us to walk in His Spirit, it's not something we force ourselves to do. It's the simple act of daily, hourly, exposing ourselves to the influence of the Holy Spirit. It's inviting the Lord into your heart, mind, body, and soul, allowing Him to permeate every action and choice of your day.

The dangerous truth is this: if the Spirit is not influencing your life holistically, you will not have dominion over sin in any area of your life. You can't separate Him out of your entertainment, relationships, words, and actions and expect

Him to be powerfully present in your struggle with lust. Our whole selves are either controlled by the Spirit or controlled by our desires.

YOUR SEXUALITY IS A WEAPON

Paul opens Romans 6 with a paragraph on the death and resurrection of Christ, illustrating that just as Christ died and rose again, so we have "died" to sin (in that we are free from it, if we choose to walk that way) and are "alive" to righteousness, fully capable of living lives pleasing to God.

He then issues a warning:

> *"Therefore do not let sin reign in your mortal body, so that you obey its desires. And do not offer any parts of it to sin as weapons of unrighteousness." (Rom. 6:12)*

Sin does not *have* to reign in our bodies. We do not *have* to be controlled by our desires. We have a choice. When we choose to sin we are offering ourselves up as sacrifices to unrighteousness. Worse yet, a lifestyle of sin becomes a *weapon* of unrighteousness, wreaking pain and separation in our own lives and in the lives of others. A weapon of sin is used to kill and destroy, which is exactly what Satan wants for the children of God (John 10:10).

But this doesn't have to be our destiny. Paul offers us hope in the very next verse:

> *"But as those who are alive from the dead, offer*

yourselves to God, and all the parts of yourselves to God as weapons for righteousness." (Rom. 6:13)

Our desires can be used for a much higher purpose than our own self-gratification: they can become weapons for righteousness. As people raised to new life in Christ we do not *have* to sin - even when our sinful nature pounds on the door. In Christ we can sacrifice our desires and use them to "fight the good fight" (1 Tim. 6:12).

So how do we choose righteousness when our desires are clamoring to be fulfilled? That depends on how much influence the Spirit of God has upon your life.

Walking by the Spirit is not a one-time decision. It's not a Sunday decision. It is a daily, hour by hour, moment by moment decision that you may have to make over and over and over until you find victory. Paul didn't say we would "rest in the Spirit" or "sit in the Spirit" or even "dwell in the Spirit". He said we would be *walking*, which indicates continual forward action. **If the Spirit of God is something you pick up in the morning, or once a week, or once a month, or never, you will be constantly overwhelmed by your desires because the Spirit of God is not overwhelming you.**

Victory is consistent when we are constantly attached, absorbed, and overwhelmed by the source of victory: Jesus Christ.

YOUR MIND IS A BATTLEFIELD

When our minds – the source of action and decision – are full of distractions and 'desire-feeders' we don't have room for the Spirit.

When devotions in the morning consist of a quick verse or passage but our minds are not focused on consuming what we read, truth is not integrated into the heart and soul. And when we don't allow the Spirit to holistically affect our lives, His power was not available when we need it most.

Many Christians live "halfway" lives that do the Christian thing without Christ's power, and in doing so they shortchange themselves. When they really need the strength of Jesus, they can't find it. But we can't blame God for being distant when it was in fact *us* who never drew near.

When I realized the battlefield of lust was in my mind, I made drastic lifestyle changes. I stopped attending the movie theater, where love stories, sex scenes and language filled my mind with images that only made me discontent. I stopped reading fiction for the same reasons. I screened my at-home movies and shows for anything that would distract me. I stopped listening to music that put my mind in a place of desire or discontent.

I learned to be *ruthless* with sin. This is what Jesus was talking about in Matthew 5:30-31:

> *"If your right eye makes you stumble, tear it out and throw it from you; for it is better for you to lose one of the parts of your body, than for your whole body to be thrown into hell. If your right hand makes you stumble, cut it off and throw it from you; for it is better for you to lose one of the parts of*

> your body, than for your whole body to go into hell."
> (Matt. 5:30-31)

Jesus wasn't telling us to literally cut off our hands and gouge out our eyes. He was saying that we are to take drastic measures when it comes to stumbling blocks in our lives. We are to be a "zero-tolerance" people with anything that hinders our spiritual walk.

> "Therefore, since we have so great a cloud of witnesses surrounding us, let us also lay aside every encumbrance and the sin which so easily entangles us, and let us run with endurance the race that is set before us, fixing our eyes on Jesus, the author and perfecter of faith..." (Hebrews 12:1-2)

We can't run the race, walk the walk, or fight the fight while entangled with anything that hinders. To get serious about having victory, we have to ask:

- What is filling my mind?
- Where are my eyes focused?
- What is keeping me from a dedicated heart, mind, and body to the Spirit of God?

Desiring relationships and sex is not "bad". But it is meant to be submitted to God, who knows our wants and needs before we even speak them.

Psalm 37:4 is my life verse. It says:

> *"Delight yourself in the Lord, and He will give you the desires of your heart."*

The desire to sin is only conquered by a desire for God – and we only desire God by delighting in Him.

RECAP:

To walk in victory, one must understand and act upon the following principles we have discussed:

- Understand your sinful desires are not God's fault, but that God wants you to pursue the desires that reflect His love and character. Pursuing God's design for all of life – especially sexuality – will produce this results.

- Allow the Spirit of God to affect your life holistically: do not divide up your life into spiritual, social, and professional. God is to be present and powerful in every part of who you are.

- Be drastic with everything that hinders you from moving forward in the Spirit of God – even if it means you lose friends, a favorite TV show, a hobby or a relationship.

- Assess what is filling your mind. For everything you remove from your mind, fill it with something positive: verse to encourage you or remind you of God's love, forgiveness, hope, and strength, songs that help you focus on Him, or other positive influences.

- Reject the thoughts when they come. I was taught that Satan cannot read minds, but he can hear our words. Speak the name of Christ when you feel overwhelmed, saying

"In the name of Jesus, I reject these thoughts." Then fill your mind with something positive.

- Remind yourself of all God has done on your behalf. I love the song by Casting Crowns that says "Who am I/that the Lord of all the earth/would care to know my name/would care to feel my hurt?" This is the perspective of gratitude.

QUESTIONS TO CONSIDER:

1. *Did it surprise you that married sex doesn't stop sexual sin? If so, why?*
2. *How can you use your sexuality as a weapon for godliness?*
3. *What drastic lifestyle changes do you need to make to align your heart, mind, and spirit with Christ in you?*

WHAT TO KNOW ABOUT THE WEDDING NIGHT

The wedding night has been both deified and demonized in Christian culture. To some, it's a destination – the conclusion of a years-long wait. For others it's a night filled less with anticipation and more with dread. In this chapter, I hope to dismantle both these expectations and share a biblical perspective on this issue.

Whether you're scared of your future wedding night or looking forward to it, the following five principles should guide your view of marital sex, particularly in the first year.

EDUCATE YOURSELF ABOUT SEXUALITY

Many young women enter their teens and twenties with very little working knowledge of sexuality. Not only do they have little knowledge of their own bodies, they don't know what sex looks like in marriage. They end up piecing together a sexual

Christian COSMO: THE SEX TALK YOU NEVER HAD

worldview from whatever sources they can find. The authorities on sexuality become Cosmo magazine, romance novels, porn sites and rumors, because when churches and parents are silent about sexuality, the world will always have a voice.

That's why a biblical sexual education is so important. I hope this book has helped you in that regard! If it has, don't let your education end here. Take this time to educate yourself: learn about your body, your hormones, the nature of sex, and why God designed you the way He did. Learn about the male body and the purpose of that design. Educate yourself about sex biologically, emotionally, and spiritually.

Why is this important? Because an inadequate sexual education leads to *fear*.

Fear and love cannot coexist, and that's especially true in the bedroom. If you are dominated by fear of sex, you won't be able to relax, trust, and rest in the love of their husband. Because sex is as much mental as it is physical, that tension will inhibit and even destroy a quality sex life. Wives must get beyond fear to truly enjoy the first night, and part of conquering such a fear is a thorough sexual education.

It is true that for many women, sex is uncomfortable at first. But in rare cases is it painful. If you expect it to be painful, there's a good chance that's exactly what will happen! For women, mental tension creates physical tension. That in turn inhibits sexual arousal and prevents the natural progression of sexual intimacy. Fear must be eradicated from your heart, mind, and bedroom, and that starts by learning what to expect.

Many girls wonder if studying sex is 'awakening love before it pleases' (Song 8:4). But God designed sexuality. If God values sexuality (and He does!) He would not expect us to ignore it, demean it, or pretend it doesn't exist until suddenly - POOF! - you're married, knowing little to nothing about sex as God designed it.

God created sex as a privilege and joy - not a duty or guilt-inducing ritual. As we embrace that truth, we mentally prepare ourselves for a wedding night of mutual love and intimacy, devoid of fear.

(Don't forget to check the resource list at the back of this book for some great books for a Christian sexual education!)

DISCUSS SEXUAL EXPECTATIONS

Discussing sexuality with your man will bring you closer on every level. These discussions should be saved for close to engagement (as opposed to early in the relationship) to keep the order of intimacy from "too much too soon". I advise discussing sex after you've been dating a while, but prior to engagement, since sexual expectations can be deal breaker.

Like worldview, our view on sexuality it colored by our education and experience. In order to have a positive sexual relationship with our spouse, we have to be completely open. Be honest about what you've done, what you look forward to and what you are uncomfortable with. Great sex is built on great trust. Honesty is necessary. It might be hard; it might be awkward; it might be uncomfortable. But it is far better to lay the cards on the table now than to find these things out on your wedding night.

This is also an opportunity to communicate your fears to the man you are marrying. If these are not communicated to him, he may never know what makes you uncomfortable and may move too fast in the excitement of the wedding night. Help him understand your feelings. Most loving, godly men will gladly alter their approach to calm the fears of their bride.

Marital sex is a journey, not a destination. If you expect your wedding night to be Hollywood, you might be disappointed. And if you expect your wedding night to be painful, you will be tense. Neither of these extremes should be our expectation. Instead, expect to give your body freely to the man you love more than anyone else in the world, and expect him to love you back in the same way. You have nothing to prove except your adoration for the man you are committing to before Almighty God.

ACCEPT GOD'S FORGIVENESS FOR SEXUAL SIN

When we refuse to accept God's forgiveness, we resist our Christ-won identity. This in turn alters our perception of love and self-worth. If you've sinned sexually in the past, in Christ you are *made new!* Don't let your former identity determine your sexual future.

Accepting God's forgiveness for past sin is a huge step in biblical intimacy. By embracing who we are in Christ, we confidently accept the love of our husbands. Insecurity cannot hold us down; we are secure in the love and grace of God. A secure woman has confidence in her body, which frees her to enjoy the accolades of her husband without disbelieving his love.

Focusing on failure destroys hope for change and reconciliation. The longer Satan keeps our eyes fixed on ourselves and our own inadequacy, the longer he keeps our eyes from the Cross. And ultimately, if you focus on sins of the past, you won't enjoy your wedding night. Focus on your CURRENT identity - as God's beloved and the beloved of your man - and be free to enjoy the sexuality He designed!

DON'T PRESSURE YOURSELF TO PERFORM

When Josh and I were first married, we felt a lot of pressure to perform sexually. We were so focused on the other person's response in the bedroom we set unrealistic expectations for one another. If our spouse didn't respond the way we expected, we both felt the weight of failure.

One day I remembered something I read in Tim Keller's book, *The Meaning of Marriage*. I don't recall the direct quote, but Tim essentially said, "Don't focus on performing for one another. Focus on loving one another as fully and completely as you can, serving one another in the bedroom, and the results will come naturally with time."

This mentality changed everything. Josh didn't want me to 'perform'. He just wanted to love me, and for me to love him.

When women go into marriage misunderstanding their husband's heart regarding sex, they accept ideals based on worldly portrayals of what men want. But if you discuss these expectations prior to entering the bedroom, you will be much better prepared to serve one another sexually.

EMBRACE THE EXCITEMENT

When our hearts our distant, our bodies aren't open to a sexual encounter. Our minds and emotions inseparable from a positive sexual experience. So when you worry about the wedding night - worry about how you look, whether your husband will like you, how well you'll "perform" – you inhibit your own sexual experience! But by trusting God's plan, embracing your identity, and accepting your husband's love, you'll jump wholeheartedly into all the excitement of marital sex.

The world has a dominated sexual conversation, and that's a terrible loss for the church. Marital sex is FUN! It should be celebrated! *You get to be excited!* Every time I go lingerie shopping, I think about how God smiles on sex done the right way. We get to enjoy it, look forward to it, delight in it, and most of all *glory* in the love of a godly husband. And as we view sex as a positive, lovely, God-blessed experience, our excitement will translate to our husbands, who will be delighted that we enjoy them so much.

Sex is good. But like anything, it takes practice. Don't burden your wedding night with unrealistic or fearful expectations - just expect to love and be loved.

QUESTIONS TO CONSIDER:

1. *What fears about the wedding night have you harbored? Bring them to Jesus right now!*

2. *Do you sense that your sexual education is sufficient? If not, look at Appendix III of this book for more resources.*

3. *If you're engaged, have you talked about sexual expectations with your fiancé? If not, set a time to do this. Make a list of questions to discuss. Also sign up for premarital counseling if you haven't already!*

HOW TO OVERCOME A SEXUAL HISTORY

"I know God has forgiven him, and I have too... but will he think differently of me? Will I be beautiful enough?"

Her question was one I asked Josh before we got married. Perhaps you've read my husband's testimony on my blog, where he told his story of God's grace and redemption over his own sexual past.

But as we approached our wedding day, I asked both Josh and God: "Will that past affect our future?"

Men and women worldwide are fighting a constant sexual barrage. Their histories range from porn addictions to molestation to rape to promiscuity. The good news of God's redemption has brought hope to ALL trapped in sexual sin and addiction – and that's something to celebrate! But like any sin, the consequences still exist, and we have a choice when it comes to the aftermath.

My blog post "Does God Forgive Sexual Sin?" talks about the

process by which God redeems us from our pasts and how to walk forward in freedom. But how do we, the spouse or significant other, walk *with* our man (or woman) into freedom? Will our own sexual past, or the past of our husbands, dictate our future happiness?

I wasn't the 'better person' of the two when Josh and I married just because I went to my wedding a virgin and he did not. We are all sinners and have fallen short of God's glory in our own way (Romans 3:23). But even though I knew he walked in God's grace, I wondered if past memories would color his perception of our sexual relationship down the road.

Are you struggling with these same thoughts? Below are five ways you can break through those doubts and walk the 'freedom road' with your boyfriend, fiancé' or husband.

ACCEPT GOD'S FORGIVENESS ON HIS BEHALF

I'm assuming that the man in question has repented of his past and is arranging his life consistently with that change of mind. If he is still struggling, I recommend the Lust Free Living book and resources as well as accountability with a male pastor, mentor or parent to help him begin the restoration process.

If his sexual history is truly behind him and he has made life changes since then, we must accept the forgiveness God extends. God has promised to forgive those who come to Him (John 1:9) and restore them to freedom, like the adulteress of John 8 ("Who condemns you?... Go and sin no more."). **When we refuse to**

forgive someone God has forgiven, we essentially place our requirement for compensation higher than God's.

We must accept the forgiveness God extends to our man and allow that forgiveness to dictate our attitudes, thoughts, and actions. This is a principle necessary in every relationship, but especially in marriage. Withholding forgiveness is a form of pride and divides us from one another. As we remember how much grace God has shown *us*, we will readily extend that same grace to those we love.

STOP COMPARING

We stand in the checkout line and wonder how, at forty years old, Drew Barrymore looks better than we do at 24. We look in the mirror and stretch out the wrinkles in our foreheads, wondering how expensive Botox is, *really*. We think about the girls our husbands dated before us and wonder… "Does he ever wish I looked like her?"

These thoughts aren't from Christ. Christ's thoughts are "true, noble, right, pure, lovely, [and] admirable" (Phil. 4:8). **Comparison is the seed of discontent .** It is the impetus to insecurity. It benefits no one – especially the person comparing herself to others.

Is it natural to compare? Definitely. I find myself doing it without intention. But just because it is *natural* does not make it *godly*, and we have to shoot it down before it takes flight. If you really think about it, comparison is a form of covetousness. **It's** not that we want what Drew Barrymore has... but we're checking to ensure we want what *we* have.

God gave us these bodies with all their quirks, lumps, bumps, spots and divets. Do I like the wrinkles on my forehead and acne scars on my face? Nope. But somehow in my genetic makeup (... and maybe because I raise my eyebrows and pick at zits) that's how I ended up. I know you've heard this a thousand times, but our bodies are the literal *temples* of God's Holy Spirit (1 Cor. 6:19). We carry the Spirit of God within us. **We are *living* arks of the covenant.**

Why compare to others, especially to the unattainable, stylized covers of magazines, when these bodies have been deemed worthy of a Holy God? Why compare to your husband's past relationships when YOU are his final choice?

Comparison destroys. Contentment unites.

RISK TRUST

Following forgiveness, we have a big decision to make. We have to give our trust.

Forgiveness is restoration. If we say we forgive but refuse to extend trust, we haven't really forgiven. We are asking the person to prove themselves to us in order to be *worthy* of our full forgiveness. **We're making them work for our grace, which is not the model Christ exemplified.**

Love is built on trust. **Sometimes trust is not earned, but given.** It's a risk we take when we love. God does this every day when He loves us: He risks the grief of our sin against Him, the pain of our unholiness – and He reaches out to love us anyway. **When we risk love by risking trust, we are living out the love of God.**

This kind of grace – undeserved trust – is motivating. **It's that feeling you get when someone believes in you no matter what you've done.** It's being a cheerleader, not a reminder of past failures. And it's hard, ladies. I know it's hard sometimes. But when I risked trust despite all past failings my husband may have made (in ANY area, not just sexually) I watched him rise to my expectation! **I believed he was more than a conqueror, and with God, that's who he became.**

Their response to trust does not rest entirely on us by any means, but by extending that vote of confidence we can do much to encourage our men to lives of victory.

BELIEVE HIM WHEN HE SAYS YOU ARE BEAUTIFUL

Let's be honest, girls: we're really hard on ourselves. We can't take compliments because we don't always believe what people say about us. We think it is vain to accept admiration for our physical, spiritual, or personal beauty. This, my friends, is insecurity. **We can only receive love when we are secure within it.**

Insecurity is a lack of trust. Just as we spoke about in the previous section, trust is necessary to relationships, and is very necessary to our relationship with God. **As we trust God, our insecurities fade and confidence in His provision takes over** our lives. This God-confidence removes all doubts and enables us to receive the love of the man God gave us.

If we can't trust God and receive His love, we can't trust our men and receive theirs. And if we refuse to receive love, we will never accept compliments on our beauty. **Overcoming our husbands' sexual past requires a heart change within ourselves.** We choose to entrust our hearts to God – who will defend and protect us (Ps. 18:1-3)– and to our men – who are commanded to love and honor us (Eph. 5:25-27) – and are then FREE to believe in that love, thrive in that protection, and forget all that lies behind (Phil. 3:13).

So choose to believe him when he says you are beautiful! Trust his words! When I discussed this with Josh, he affirmed to me that past images and relationships were no comparison to the beautiful, holy, God-ordained relationship he has with me now. I am beautiful to him because he knows and loves me. He doesn't look for flaws or compare me to past images – images and scenarios with which he has no loving relationship.

By rejecting his admiration, all I do is hurt *myself* and discourage my man. When we keep telling our men, "No, I'm not beautiful." Or "You're wrong, I'm fat!" we're telling them they *shouldn't* appreciate us as we are. We are rejecting their efforts to love us! **So trust God's identity for you (1 Peter 2) trust your man's love for you, and believe him when he says you are beautiful.**

SUPPORT, AFFIRM, AND ENCOURAGE HIS WALK WITH GOD

Let your love unite you.

Whether you are dating, engaged, or married, let your mutual love of Christ and your love for each other bring you ever closer. When you are tempted to doubt God's love or doubt your husband's – run to Scripture and see what God says about who you are and how you are loved. **No man can ever fulfill us because no man was ever meant to – only God can do that.**

But as we draw near to God and trust His unwavering love for us, we begin to understand grace a little better. And as we understand grace better, we can give it much more freely.

Grace-based relationships are God's intention. Be your man's cheerleader! Give him grace, and by that grace teach him what true trust and love looks like. **Believe in the redemption that covers him, and let his story be a testimony to many still trapped in sexual sin.**

HOW TO CONFESS YOUR OWN PAST

But what if you're the one confessing a history of sin? Let's talk about what that looks like.

SET A DIRECTION

Sharing about a history of sin, sex, and shame is no easy task. It shouldn't be taken lightly or shared too quickly. That's why it's very important to come to this conversation with a vision for what you wish to accomplish. Pray for the right timing and the right words – God promises to give them (Luke 12:12)!

To set a direction for the conversation, take note of the following:

- **The stage of your relationship.** Sharing too early (before knowing one another's true intentions) can cause further emotional trauma. Sharing too late (after engagement) can be a deal breaker for some couples.

- **What you plan to share.** Have an idea of what you will tell your boyfriend and in what order you will tell it. If you know this will be an emotional experience for you, perhaps write it down in letter form.

- **Your end goal.** What do you hope to accomplish by sharing about your past? Be sure that you are not seeking freedom, healing, or spiritual redemption through the relationship itself. It should also be noted that your boyfriend (or girlfriend) **should not** be your accountability partner for any sexual struggle. They are too close to you and to the situation. Find someone of the same gender, preferably older and/or more spiritually mature, to fill that role.

BE HONEST BUT DISCREET

This is where it gets tricky. We should never begin a relationship in dishonesty – hiding things destroys trust, which in turn prevents intimacy. But there are many details that are better left untold. This requires that we be *honest* but also *discreet.* What does that look like, practically speaking?

- **Share generalities.** If you slept with a previous boyfriend, if you struggle with masturbation, if you had a problem with porn in the past – these are things your boyfriend should know if you are moving toward engagement. Sexual sin is not an "easy fix" and as such often pops back up in a different form, even if you've conquered it on the past. If you struggled with lust as a single woman, you may be tempted by lust in your relationship – in fact, I can almost guarantee that. By telling your boyfriend the area of your past struggles, you can join forces to fight against temptation in your relationship.

- **Do not share specifics, even if asked.** Your boyfriend does not need to know what *exactly* you did with your last relationship. When we describe the details of sexual sins, we not only resurrect those images in our own minds but implant them into our partner's. These thoughts and images often result in such insecurity and doubt they destroy many otherwise wonderful relationships.

- **Discuss expectations.** If you and/or your partner are headed toward marriage, use this opportunity to discuss expectations (this is not a conversation that should be had early in a relationship, as it bonds a couple too soon). Given your respective sexual histories, is there anything about sex that scares you? Is there anything you know would be an issue in marriage? Have you been through counseling for these things? Are you in agreement concerning sexuality? Are you at peace with what you know about one another's pasts?

This conversation is not easy. I remember when Josh and I had this discussion; I felt horribly awkward, nervous, and scared. But I also knew that God's grace was over me, and that in Him I had forgiveness. Josh knew that too. We extended to one another the grace that Christ had extended to us, and it strengthened us for the battle against lust we fought throughout our dating relationship. Most importantly, our honesty laid a foundation of trust for our future marriage. Though we continue to pursue purity in our marriage – checking on one another and tending to that trust foundation – we make sure to have people outside of our relationship to offer insight and advice as our journey continues. (Outside accountability and/or counseling is always a good idea.)

TAKE ACTION

Once you've had the conversation, it's time to put that knowledge to use. If you one or both have you have struggled with sexual sin, you will need to be *on guard* to protect the purity of your relationship. Making rules and setting standards won't work on their own, because lust is a sin issue, not a sex issue. That's why we should stop asking "how far is too far?"

Remember: virginity is not God's goal – holiness is. Even if your past has left you with scars, remember that scars are a sign of healing. God has done and will continue to do a redemptive work in you, if you walk in His design for sexuality. He is the Protector of relationships, the Redeemer of our pain, and the Hope for the not-so-good girl.

QUESTIONS TO CONSIDER:

1. *If you partner has a sexual past, has he repented? If so, do you still struggle to accept that he has a sexual past? Begin by praying that God would open your heart to receive and give grace in this area.*

2. *Do you regularly compare yourself to your partner's past? This will destroy your relationship! Begin recognizing comparison and taking those thoughts captive as soon as they enter your mind.*

3. *Have you and your partner discussed these issues honestly (but not with unnecessary details)? If not, have the discussion soon. But once over, do not rehash the discussion or bring it back up unless you are hoping to resolve a specific issue. Allow Christ to deal with your insecurities – your partner will never fix them. Finally, get counseling if you are still struggling.*

THE TRUTH ABOUT FANTASIZING

For the majority of my high school years *every* relationship I had was a fantasy relationship: it simply didn't exist. While I had committed not to date in high school so I could focus on my academic and extracurricular goals, I made up plenty of scenarios in my head. I imagined a less awkward version of myself holding conversations with the guys I liked. I was always dressed perfectly. He always said nice things. It was *just like the movies.* That's why the young man at the concert nearly shocked my socks off – he was a dream come true.

I rehearsed these scenarios with every guy I liked, to the point that when I actually saw those boys I was bewildered about what to say. **Because I had trained my mind to view them as prospects – not as human beings and brothers in Christ – I also overthought every action they took.** I painstakingly examined our conversations to look for hints that they "liked" me. It was all very exhausting, as well as fruitless – considering I met my husband a good eight years later.

Now that I'm married to a wonderful man, I almost can't believe how much mental energy was expended on relationships that didn't exist in my single years. While "fantasizing" (innocently or sexually – though sexual fantasizing is more spiritually dangerous, it almost always begins innocently) seems harmless, there are several factors that make it a poor choice for single women:

FANTASY GLAMORIZES REALITY

What's the harm in imagining a conversation with the man of your dreams? Nothing, really – if that's where it stays. But the mind is a powerful thing: Creating thoughts that become actions, actions that become habit, and habits that can become character. Fantasizing – creating imaginary situations and conversations – glamorizes reality. Fantasizing allows us to control a relationship that does not exist. It sets up expectations that are often disappointed in day-to-day interaction, and damages the development of what could be a healthy, genuine relationship.

In our dreams, we can control what the other person is saying, what we are wearing, and the outcome of the fantasy. That's not the case in reality. Fantasizing sets expectations that no man can fulfill, setting girls up for disappointment down the road.

FANTASY ENCOURAGES DISCONTENT

When you're in a relationship, fantasy takes a backseat. You already *have* a relationship; you don't need to dream about it! Of course, within relationships there are other struggles – the battle for mental purity WILL continue, just on a different level. But for single girls, fantasy usually takes the form of imagining a relationship they do not yet have. If you spend a good deal of time on this topic, the only result is discontent.

Because fantasy concentrates on something we do not have, it directs our minds into envy and unhappiness. A steady diet of "relationship imagination" will leave you more unhappy than when you began, wondering why you don't have a relationship, where you can get one, and eventually ending in an urgency that often leads girls to make foolish, impulsive decisions in dating. Contentment has no room to live in a mind consumed with fantasy, because contentment *requires acceptance of the reality we've been given.*

FANTASY IS A DISTRACTION

Our minds have only so much energy for what we need to do each day. All of us have responsibilities: work, school, family, home. Fantasizing is attractive because it takes us away from reality – temporarily. Fantasy is a *distraction* from real life in every sense. It is a world of imagination, not intentional thinking.

Intentional thinking, by contrast, results in intentional living. When we live intentionally we end up acting intentionally and making decisions that are fruitful and beneficial to our future. But a mind consumed with fantasy is not prepared for what is ahead.

One of the reasons I stopped reading fiction in my teens was because of the above. Fiction – outside of some historical classics – in today's world is largely focused on relationships. I found that no matter what I read as a single woman I ran into these fictional relationships, which added to the scenarios I entertained in my mind. The more I read, the more discontent I became. I also realized my expectations on real men – like, men who aren't in novels – were unrealistically altered by what I saw in these books. Secular fiction went so far as to include sex scenes, but Christian novels weren't much better. So for the last 7 years, I have gone without fiction (for the most part – I've tried a few novels here and there) for the sake of holiness and contentment. It was my "How holy?" moment.

HOW FANTASY DAMAGES REAL RELATIONSHIPS

As previously mentioned, fantasizing damages real relationships by setting up false expectations. "Romance culture" – the perfect storylines we see in movies and books – has us thinking we need that in real relationship. When a man doesn't act the way these media sources say he should, we write him off as "lazy" or "not hot/smart/charming enough". Good men aren't always good looking. Good men aren't always the smartest in the room. And good men aren't always perfectly charming in every respect.

But good men love God, love people, and work hard to win the heart of the women they adore. Romance comes as love is built. Sadly, fantasy can cause a woman to overlook what could have been a wonderful relationship – all because the guy doesn't measure up to the storyline she's formulated in her head.

Not only can fantasy cause young women to ignore an otherwise godly young man, it can make her *consider* an unworthy one simply because he is charming, handsome, or presents a movie-like relationship storyline. If I hadn't snapped out of my "this is really happening" trance with the guy at the concert, I may have considered him based on nothing more than the romance of the moment.

FANTASY WEAKENS OUR MINDS FOR THE BATTLE

Finally, and most seriously, fantasizing about relationships and potential mates weakens our minds for the battles ahead. **Fantasy is a hiding place.** It is neither real nor wholesome. It is not directed toward positive action, nor in worship of God. And it trains our minds to focus on something we don't have, while missing out on all that we do.

1 Peter 1:13 says: "Therefore, **prepare your minds for action, keep sober in spirit, fix your hope completely on the grace to be brought to you at the revelation of Jesus Christ."**

This verse is so powerful! We cannot fantasize about relationships and simultaneously prepare our minds for action. We can't be sober in spirit when our hearts are drunk on the idea of an idealistic romance. And we cannot fix our hope COMPLETELY on Christ when it's already fixed on a girlish crush. **We must control our minds.**

It is one thing to pray for your future husband, to have dreams, and indulge in a once-in-a-while glance at the future. It's another to allow our hearts and minds to be consumed with love, romance, and the idea of a relationship that does not yet exist. **The simple truth is that where your mind is focused is where your heart will go.** Satan uses "good" things to distract us from what is best. What is best is to cultivate a mind that is dedicated to Christ, and therefore actions that reflect His power.

If we are to overcome fantasy, we have to stop those thoughts and habits in their tracks. It won't be easy – especially if you've been doing it a long time. **For each thought you "take captive", replace it with a promise of God.** Rehearse the qualities in God that you were trying to find in imaginary relationships – His love, protection, kindness, His gentlemanliness. **Because God is a gentleman.** He doesn't force us to follow Him – He opens His hand, extending it toward us, asking us to walk with Him. We choose whether or not to go.

QUESTIONS TO CONSIDER:

1. Do you make a habit of fantasizing about crushes, actors, musicians, or fictional characters? This is inhibiting your walk with God and your future relationships. Begin taking captive these thoughts and redirecting them into prayer.

2. What are three things you can pray about every time you're tempted to fantasize?

3. What books and media do you need to stop consuming in order to honor God with your thoughts?

PREACH THE GOSPEL WITH YOUR SEXUALITY

We hear about purity in the context of sex and marriage, but purity isn't just about sex. Purity is not about you or me. It's bigger than that.

Purity is a lifestyle; it influences every choice we make. By pigeon-holing purity as a sexual issue, we've missed God's intentions when He called us to holiness. When God said "Be holy as I am holy", He wasn't being arbitrary. Holiness is how we know God and make Him known – which is our entire purpose in this world! God expects purity from all who claim the name of Christ, but sometimes we forget *why* we need it.

So if you've ever wondered why purity matters, this is for you.

YOUR PURITY POINTS TO GOD'S GRACE

Therefore, since we have these promises, dear friends, let us purify ourselves from everything that contaminates body and spirit, perfecting holiness out of reverence for God. (2 Cor. 7:1)

We are not pure by anything we personally have done. All of us are born into sin, unable to make ourselves pure enough to commune with God. The hopeless state of humanity is why Jesus came to bridge the gap between us and God. Our imputed holiness came at the highest of costs. We are made pure by the blood of Christ – and are now responsible to live up to that identity.

The purity of our lives points to the grace of God, and how seriously we regard it reveals how much we appreciate God's grace! When we make excuses for compromised living, the real problem is in our hearts. Impure lives point to hearts that don't appreciate what God did through Jesus.

The more we comprehend God's grace, the more we long for purity – and the more we share that grace with our world.

YOUR PURITY PROVES GOD'S POWER

But just as he who called you is holy, so be holy in all you do; for it is written: "Be holy, because I am holy." (1 Pet. 1:15-16)

Purity isn't just about sex, but here's an important truth: If you don't pursue purity in every area of life, you'll struggle to uphold it sexually. Because holiness isn't something we only pursue in *one* area of life, we can't expect to honor God sexually when we refuse to reverence Him in our friendships, entertainment, and spare time.

Our purity proves the power of God. If God is truly all-good and all-mighty, our lives should reflect that, but we will only reflect the influential power of Christ if we align ourselves with His will. God's power is evident in us to the degree we obey Him. We obey Him by *choosing purity.*

YOUR PURITY ATTESTS TO GOD'S LOVE

He has saved us and called us to a holy life—not because of anything we have done but because of his own purpose and grace. This grace was given us in Christ Jesus before the beginning of time. (2 Tim. 1:9)

This holy life we're called to live is *all* because of God's grace. Remember: It cost God *everything* to make you holy. When you choose to live below that calling – making excuses for compromise and cultural ideals – you're spurning the identity Jesus died to provide.

Your purity, then, attests to the love of God. The more you embrace holiness in your life, the more you proclaim the love of God to your community. You reveal that knowing God *makes a difference.* Knowing Christ *changes lives.* People will notice, but only if you prioritize purity the way God does. As you do, His love will be made evident in your every sphere of influence.

YOUR PURITY GIVES HOPE TO THE WORLD

Make every effort to live in peace with everyone and to be holy; without holiness, no one will see the Lord. (Heb. 12:14)

Without holiness, *no one will see the Lord.* This verse sums up the importance of purity. Holiness is not optional. It is a requirement of Christian living. The purity of our lives offers hope to a dying world: Hope that lasting impact is possible. Hope that life has purpose. Hope for an eternity after death.

Purity keeps us in a peaceful, powerful relationship with God. But is also our primary witness to the world! It is our purity that reveals God's intentions for every man and woman on earth. Our lives evangelize more than our words ever could, and how purely we live is our loudest proclamation of the gospel.

YOUR PURITY HAS ETERNAL CONSEQUENCE

Therefore, I urge you, brothers and sisters, in view of God's mercy, to offer your bodies as a living sacrifice, holy and pleasing to God—this is your true and proper worship. (Rom. 12:1)

Purity has a cost: It is uncomfortable, unpopular, and difficult at times. Purity is why I no longer wear leggings as pants, don't watch many TV shows, and rarely read fiction. I don't refrain because these things are inherently evil. These choices are the product of spiritual maturity: The closer I press to the heart of God, the less I think of my Christian "liberty" and the more seriously I take my Christian *responsibility*.

This life is not about my desires, as much as I'd often like to fulfill them. This life is my one chance to proclaim the gospel. My purity matters – *and so does yours.* Your purity is a chance to fulfill the Great Commission right where you are.

Every decision matters for the gospel of Christ. You are a missionary, whether you wear that title or not – and *your purity proclaims the gospel.*

What kind of gospel does it preach?

QUESTIONS TO CONSIDER:

1. *How does the knowledge that your purity is your evangelism affect how you view sexuality?*

2. *What are some ways you will "preach the gospel" with your sexuality?*

3. *How can your sexuality draw you closer to God this year? This month? Today?*

ACKNOWLEDGEMENTS

To my husband Josh, thank you for always supporting my work with your presence and wisdom. You truly are my "co-laborer in Christ" and I am ever grateful for your input and support. Thank you also for being my tech-guy, my coffee supplier, and a constant sounding board.

To my family, particularly my sister Autumn, thank you for letting me talk through these ideas and share a journey that involves your stories as well as mine. Mom and Dad, thanks for setting me up for success and grounding my childhood in Christ so I could navigate these topics as I got older.

To Jennifer White, thank you for your wisdom, guidance, mentorship, and editorial eye! I am so grateful to have met you and learn from you as a true Titus 2 woman.

To Shaunti Feldhahn, thank you for the research and wisdom shared in each of your books, which greatly influenced my own perspective on sexuality.

To Juli Slattery, who does not know me but who has had a profound influence on my work and ministry: thank you for all you do through Authentic Intimacy. I pray many men and women continue to be touched by what you do.

And for Adeline, my daughter: I pray your perspective on your femininity will be grounded in God's design from the very beginning.

APPENDIX I

I WAITED UNTIL MY WEDDING NIGHT TO LOSE MY VIRGINITY, AND IT'S THE BEST THING I EVER DID

I got the text from my friend while I was sipping coffee in a renovated cottage-turned-cafe. It contained a link.

"This writer did a purity pledge," The texts continued. "And has rejected all of it. You need to read it, and some of the comments."

So I did, and as tears welled in my eyes, I knew I'd have to do what I *really* don't like doing: write a response post.

The article was entitled "It Happened to Me: I Waited Until My Wedding Night to Lose My Virginity and I Wish I Hadn't." I read it in its entirety. The more I read, the more heartbroken I felt for Samantha (the author) and the twisted experience she relayed in the post. But my sadness was overwhelmed with a sense of utter urgency.

A lot of young women will read that post: young women who have made purity pledges and are waiting for an excuse to walk away from them. Young women teetering on the brink of sexual and spiritual destruction. Young women wondering if it is even *worth* this waiting-for-marriage.

Waiting for marriage to lose my virginity was the best decision

I ever made. At times it was difficult. I wanted to give up. Yet I'm going to battle for the other side because this waiting-for-marriage thing – it's worth it, even when the choice is hard.

Sometimes it was an uphill battle against this culture we live in, but I was able to keep my commitment to sexual holiness. Here's why:

1. My commitment to purity wasn't to a church: it was to Christ Himself.

Samantha was either coerced or convinced into committing to a purity pledge in front of her entire church. This was the first mistake of her parents and her church at large.

We should not be committing to purity for the sake of a church. We should commit to purity for the sake of Christ. When we make spiritual commitments for mortal and material reasons, those commitments have no authoritative standard.

My commitment to purity was encouraged by my parents, but it was MY decision. I had to decide why I was committing to this. I had to decide whether or not to wear a purity ring. I had to decide who I was doing this for: myself, my parents, a man, or God?

I struggled with that decision. At times I DID take pride in my purity, but I soon realized my purity was not 'my purity'. It's God's, and I'm doing it for Him or it's not worth anything at all.

2. My spiritual identity, not my sexual identity, determined my life choices.

If we make life choices based on only one part of our being

– mental, physical, sexual – when those variable entities are altered by time and circumstance, our choices will be worthless.

Saving my virginity was a spiritual decision. Because it was a spiritual decision that affected my sexuality (not a sexual decision that affected my spirit), my whole life fell into step with my spiritual worldview. I wanted to be pure because my spirit was in line with Jesus Christ, who is the essence of purity.

3. My commitment to purity was not because it's 'my body, my choice'.

In her article, Samantha told her boyfriend she committed to purity and he respected that decision because it was 'her body, her choice'. But what about when you decide 'your body' wants to have sex? If it is your choice alone, there is no standard higher than your own autonomy.

I made a commitment to purity because I am God's child, and my body and choices were aligned with His loving will. Because I answer to Someone greater than myself, Someone I trust knows sex and the way to use it, I used it the way He says to. I waited until marriage.

God was good for His promise, and it's been great!

As a Christian woman, my body is NOT my own (1 Cor. 6:19-20). I have been bought with the blood of a Savior. Every sexually-demeaning choice I make I consequently demean the blood of the Son of God. So because I valued Jesus, I valued His standard for sex. And I waited.

4. My failure to act purely in relationships prior to

marriage brought me great guilt and shame, but that guilt drove me to repentance and a change of lifestyle – not a change of God's sexual standards.

While I did go to the altar a virgin, I made mistakes in my dating relationships. I had one relationship with a man who threatened to leave me if I didn't alter my physical standards. Having never faced anything of this nature, I allowed myself to be manipulated and gave more than I had hoped to give. I have never felt so guilty and used.

I could have decided that the guilt came from a lack of sexual identity. I could have told myself what I did wasn't actually wrong – that it was just me being silly and inexperienced. If I had believed those lies, stayed with that man and given more than I did, I may not have had the beautiful love story I do today.

The guilt could have driven me to justify sin and change God's sexual standards, but instead the guilt drove me to repentance. Because I know I have an Advocate in heaven (Heb. 4:11), because I know I am God's child whom He loves (Jn. 1:12), and because I know I can approach the throne of grace to ask forgiveness (1 Jn. 1:9) I brought my sin to God and was reconciled to Him. He saved me from destroying myself and my love story.

We do not get to determine God's sexual standards. Should you be naked with each other before marriage? No. Should your boyfriend have his hands in your shirt? No. Should you be 'making out' on the couch but sitting in the pew the next morning without a qualm? No.

We shouldn't allow ourselves to demean sexuality this way.

We should make <u>every effort</u> to keep a high value on something that God values SO MUCH he requires marriage for participation in it.

5. My commitment to purity made sex an exciting part of marriage to which I looked forward with anticipation.

The environment in which Samantha was taught about sex is the chief contributor to her painful experience. Sex was taught as 'bad' until her wedding night, when you say some vows and sex is instantly 'good'. My experience was far different.

Sex was a *good thing* before and after marriage; but I only participated in it AFTER my vows. Sex was never a 'bad' thing. My parents never whispered about it or acted as if it were taboo. I heard it preached about from the pulpit on occasions. I was taught about it in my youth group. The message was not, "Sex is bad! Stay away from it or you will be punished!" The message was, "Sex is wonderful, great, and God-designed – but it's not time yet. Honor God and ensure the best sexual experience by waiting until marriage."

So I looked forward to that experience. I knew it would be a learning curve. It wouldn't be 'Hollywood' the first time or couple of times – that was true!

But sex was not evil: it was of high value. I was not taught to avoid sex out of guilt, but to protect it from being cheapened. And that's how it was on my wedding night: an experience of the greatest value.

6. My wedding night was neither awkward nor guilt-rid-

den. I felt safe, loved, honored, and adored by my husband and my God.

Yes, it was physically uncomfortable. Yes, it was new. But contrary to the girl in the aforementioned article, I didn't cry in the bathroom afterwards, and I didn't feel dirty, guilty, or used. .

My sexual relationship with my husband remains a joy to me, not because we're masters or we know it all; not because we get it perfect every time. It was and is a joy because we are progressing in a pure, God-blessed love. I have no memories of anyone but him. I have no insecurities based on comparison to the past.

I am secure in my relationship with a Lord who loves me regardless of how my husband loves me, and because my husband treats me the way God has commanded him (with tenderness and care) I am continually surrounded by security and love.

7. My virginity did not determine my salvation. It was a product of my love for God.

The writer of this article says, "If I had it over, I would have sex before marriage, and I wouldn't go to hell for it."

Correction: We don't go to Hell for sex before marriage. We go to Hell for rejecting Jesus Christ, who gives us laws of holiness out of His incredible love.

My virginity was not the determination of my faith. It was a product of my faith. I didn't even *think* about my virginity, in fact; for the most part, I simply lived life learning how to be a woman of God. My parents poured into me. My youth leaders discipled me. My love for God and my desire to be a woman who reflected His goodness was my motivator. I protected my virginity because I loved God: plain and simple.

8. My sexual identity is inseparably tied to my identity in Christ.

The author of the article says, "Your sexuality is nobody's business but yours." False. If you claim to be a Christian woman (and frankly, even if you don't) your sexuality is God's business because He designed *you* and He designed sex.

Sexual identity is front and center in this culture, which is actually quite demeaning since we are each so much more than a sexual object. But you, young woman: your identity is so much more than who you are sexually. God knows that. God wants to make you holistically the best person you can possibly be – not just the best person you can sexually become.

I was taught this principle. Because of it, my virginity was only a minor part of my Christian faith. Virginity, and waiting for marriage to give it up, was not a burden but an honor to me. It was as if God had bestowed on me a great gift to carry for however many years – a gift I would open when I reached 'the finish line'. The more I ripped off the gift on the journey the less I'd have when I arrived.

And how, if I opened the gift too soon, would that be *God's* fault?

The moments where I ceased to trust God's goodwill and love *for me* were where I made my greatest mistakes. God's design is for our glory and our protection, not a spoiling of the 'real deal'.

Samantha says little girls want to believe in fairy tales, so I say: give them a fairy tale. Give them a God-ordained fairy tale, the beauty of a girl unbroken, unused, and unhurt. When Samantha moralizes sex before marriage, she recommends heartache, brokenness, promiscuity, and potential abuse.

She is saying *self* is greater than God; that God doesn't know what He is doing. That when God designed sex, He had no clue where it would best be used.

Despite the fact she has never experienced a man using her, leaving her, taking her virginity and dumping her like a rag doll, her post suggests sex before marriage would have been the better choice.

Her words are those of a culture that thinks it knows sex better than God does, and *girls will listen to her.*

Don't listen to her or any of the lies propagated by that post.

Let me tell you what true sexual freedom is: it is the freedom, on your wedding night, of knowing there is no longer any boundary. It is the freedom of knowing you are loved and protected. It is the freedom of pure, ecstatic appreciation of your beauty. It is the freedom of knowing the man in bed with you will not be gone in the morning.

God knows sex better than anyone else. His design is meant for love and protection. Follow that design, and it will be the best choice you ever make.

APPENDIX II

BIRTH CONTROL

This is an issue that requires prayer and thoughtful consideration, as well as discussion with your fiancé or husband. However, it's also a topic on which few resources are provided from a Christian perspective. As an engaged woman, I found only two extremes: those who believe in no birth control whatsoever and those who pop a pill, no questions asked. So what options are available? There are actually quite a few.

THE PILL, RINGS, SHOTS AND PATCHES

Most, if not all of these are hormone-based. Here is a description from WebMD:

"These hormones work to inhibit the body's natural cyclical hormones to prevent pregnancy. Pregnancy is prevented by a combination of factors. The hormonal contraceptive usually stops the body from ovulating. Hormonal contraceptives also change the cervical mucus to make it difficult for the sperm to go through the cervix and find an egg. Hormonal contraceptives can also prevent pregnancy by changing the lining of the womb so it's unlikely the fertilized egg will be implanted."

CONDOMS

- A blockade method used by the husband (although female condoms are manufactured).

DIAPHRAGM AND SPERMICIDE

- The diaphragm, like the condom, is a blockade method used by the wife instead of the husband, negating the need for a condom. Spermicide is used in conjunction with it to prevent fertilization.

WITHDRAWAL METHOD

- Described here (I didn't want to articulate that myself! LOL!)

FAMILY PLANNING/CALENDAR METHOD

- This method is based on an ovulation calendar, a woman with a regular cycle and sometimes body temperature used to gauge when it is 'safe' to be intimate. This method is often used by families opposed to other forms of birth control. Here is a short description.

WHY I <u>PERSONALLY</u> NEVER USE THE PILL:
HEALTH

I have always had issues with my feminine health. I have long cycles, usually 8-14 day long periods, and cramps so bad I can feel them in my toes. Every doctor I've seen has tried to put me on the pill for acne, cramping, and regulating cycles. The truth is that the pill does not resolve these issues; it simply covers them up. In many cases, taking hormonally based birth control pills will exacerbate a hormonal imbalance, causing further health issues (and even infertility) down the road. Details regarding this are contained in the book *WomanCode* by Alisa Vitti, which I recommend to every woman!

Pumping additional hormones into my body for an indeterminate amount of time is not appealing to me. Of my married friends, *fifteen* of them are now off the pill for the following reasons: migraines, weight gain, weight loss, mood swings, lack of libido, pain during sex, and inability to *have* sex. All of those are risks I don't want to take.

FAITH

I'll talk about this more in a bit, but when I sat down with Josh to discuss this topic we looked to the Word for our guidance. Everywhere in Scripture that family or children are mentioned, it is clear that children are close to God's heart. He continually tells His people to 'be fruitful and multiply', while also promising to provide for their 'children's children' and be faithful to them 'generation after generation'. We prayed about our decision, and came to the conclusion that hormonally altering my body was contrary to God's design for the family, marriage, and his design of my body as a woman. We want to be ready to accept a baby at any time, but we also have financial obligations at this time. So with prayer, we decided that a combination of condoms, diaphragm, withdrawal AND family planning would work for us. We change it up depending on the calendar, and have been at peace with that decision.

MORALITY

Most birth control pills on the market today contain an abortive back up much like the "morning after" pill. Even if the pill doesn't have that 'back up', the hormones of the pill can both prevent ovulation and in some cases, thin the uterine lining, preventing implantation. What does this mean?

It means that if life begins at conception, a fertilized egg could travel to the uterus, attempt to implant, but starve to death because the uterine lining is too thin. It could take up to 10 days for the egg to finally die off. As Christians, we need to take this into consideration if we proclaim that we are genuinely pro-life.

GOD'S VIEW AND VISION FOR CHILDREN

Our God loves children (Psalm 127:3-5). Jesus loved children (Matt. 19:14). **But our culture, and even our churches, tells**

us that children are either interruptions or little idols. We put them off as long as possible, only to worship them when they arrive.

Life doesn't 'end' when you have kids. They add a lot of responsibility, yes – but they become part of life itself, not a hindrance to it! So when choosing birth control, cultivate the same level of appreciation for children that God does. He understands that you may want to have a year with just you and your husband; and you can tell Him that. But do not despise that which God loves.

A few verses to consider:

- As Christians we are to offer our bodies as a living sacrifice. *Romans 12:1*

- Children are a reward from the Lord. *Psalm 127.3*

- God is able to open and close the womb. *Genesis 30:22; 1 Samuel 1:5*

- God knows us before we are even born. *Jeremiah 1:5; Hebrews 7:10*

Read more here.

WHAT ABOUT JUDAH AND TAMAR?

The account of Genesis 38, between Judah and Tamar is truly the only reference to birth 'control' in all of Scripture; this is because the culture in which Scripture was written (both Old and New Testaments) was very different from ours. Children were a legacy and a blessing, not something to avoid. The more children, the stronger the family.

In the Genesis 38 account, the issue was not that Tamar's brothers-in-law used the pull-out method. The issue was that they were disobeying God's law, stated in Deuteronomy 25:5-7 "When brothers live together and one of them dies and has no son, the wife of the deceased shall not be married outside the family to a strange man. Her husband's brother shall go in to her and take her to himself as wife and perform the duty of a husband's brother to her." By denying Tamar a son, they were not fulfilling their responsibility according to Mosaic Law.

As Christians, we are no longer bound to Mosaic Law (See Romans 5-7). Our brothers do not marry the wives of their deceased brethren. However, the principle at play here – the issue of taking responsibility for your family – still stands. The Old Testament provides context for New Testament commands, but it is the New Testament (new covenant) to which we are bound. Paul states this in 1 Tim. 5:8 when he says, "But if anyone does not provide for his own, and especially for those of his household, he has denied the faith and is worse than an unbeliever."

Thus, Gen. 38 is not about birth control, but familial responsibility – another reason we should be considering our finances early on in preparation for children – whether or not we have them right away.

GOD'S VIEW AND VISION FOR FINANCES

Phil. 4:19 says, **"My God shall supply all your need ac-**

cording to his riches in glory by Christ Jesus." It is illogical to assume that Paul is only talking about spiritual provision here; for like Jesus says in Matthew 7:10 **"Which one of you... if [your son] asks for a fish, would you give him a stone?... If you then, being evil, know how to give good gifts to your children, how much more will your Father who is in heaven give what is good to those who ask Him!"** (Matt. 7:11) God supplies our every need – but not always our every want.

We are an entitled generation. We think we deserve the life our parents have *now*, when they didn't start out that way! My parents started out in a trailer park with a car and a dream, and made a beautiful life out almost nothing. My husband and I both have great jobs, a beautiful apartment and a nice vehicle, all at 24 years old. We have been given everything we both *need* and *want*. This in mind, it is our responsibility to steward God's gifts with the future in mind – and that includes children.

Financial responsibility is a biblical principle. **Proverbs 21:20** says, "Precious treasure and oil are in a wise man's dwelling, but a foolish man devours it." In other words – he spends everything he earns, with no eye to the future.

Proverbs 22:3 states: "The prudent see danger and take refuge, but the simple keep going and pay the penalty." Mr. M and I have asked ourselves: are we a prudent couple? Are we prudent parents *now*, before we have kids? Those habits don't just happen! They must be cultivated from the beginning. We used Dave Ramsey's <u>Financial Peace University</u> while we were dating, and it has been fantastic.

BIRTH CONTROL IS A MUTUAL DECISION

If you are a Christian woman, this is not a 'my body, my choice' decision. If that's your view, Planned Parenthood would applaud you.

This is a decision between you and God and between you and your husband. You are God's designed woman; the crowning glory of creation! And you will be your husband's wife, who will be the father of your future children. He has a say in this decision, so truly consult and pray together as you navigate these choices.

YOUR PERSONAL HEALTH AND WELL-BEING

What is best for your body? Your gynecologist gets paid for every prescription she writes, so research what she is trying to give you. Look into the side effects, and don't just take it because she says it will work.

Keep in mind that you are the one who calls the shots on your body; not the doctor. Come into the office informed so you can determine what you are looking for (the gynecologist can prescribe the diaphragm, by the way, which is my favorite method that we use).

Also remember that your body is the temple of the Holy Spirit, and only choose options that allow you to live that out with freedom and vitality.

FAITH CANNOT BE SHORTCUT

Children require a lot of faith: faith for provision, faith for health, faith for strength, faith for wisdom. Children can bring uncertainty, yes – but uncertainty requires dependency on God, and that's exactly what He wants of us. No more of this 'I can do it myself', 'Ew, kids! Never ever!' ingratitude our culture propagates and even the church embraces. Faith is required of us. We can expect it, embrace it, and build our lives around it.

All of God's gospel story, and all of God's laws, are an A + B + C progression: I have faith in God's provision, protection, wisdom and strength; therefore, I steward my finances as gifts from Him; I expect Him to give me all I need; I seek Him for wisdom in all that I do; I trust Him to give me the strength I need for whatever comes. Will it be hard? Possibly. Jesus said, "In the world you will have tribulation." (John 16:33) and Peter repeated it: "Beloved, do not be surprised at the fiery ordeal among you, which comes upon you for your testing, as though some strange thing were happening to you..."(1 Peter 4:12)

But in those same verses, we hear Jesus saying, "... But take heart; I have overcome the world." And Peter echoes this, saying: "but to the degree that you share the sufferings of Christ, keep on rejoicing, so that also at the revelation of His glory you may rejoice with exultation....

For us, our decision is the middle road of birth control: not telling God what's what, but not seeking a child at this present time. Our hands were open to God's timing – and he surprised us with our first daughter more quickly than we thought!- and He proved sufficient for our every need. Prayerfully approach Him with your own decision, and He'll guide you in the right path.

APPENDIX III

HELPFUL RESOURCES

Below is a list of my recommended websites, books, and authors to further enhance your study of biblical sexuality:

BOOKS AND MINISTRIES:

- Authentic Intimacy Ministries: Dr. Juli Slattery and Linda Dillow
    - Java with Juli Podcast
    - *25 Questions About Love, Sex, and Intimacy* by Juli Slattery
    - *Pulling Back the Shades* by Juli Slattery
    - *Sex and the Single Woman* by Juli Slattery
- Lust Free Living Ministries
    - *Unveil: Lust Free Living* - A must-read for any woman struggling with sexual sin. Use the discount code "delta" at checkout.
- God Over Porn Ministry
- *Sex and the Soul of a Woman* by Paula Rinehart

- *Return to Modesty* by Wendy Shalit
- *Intended for Pleasure* by Ed and Gaye Wheat
- *Sex is Not the Problem: Lust Is* by Josh Harris
- *For Women Only* by Shaunti Feldhahn
- *Through a Man's Eyes* by Shaunti Feldhahn
- *Romancing Your Husband* by Debra White Smith
- *The Good Girl's Guide to Great Sex* by Sheila Wray Gregoire
- *Intimate Issues* by Linda Dillow
- *Kissed the Girls and Made Them Cry* by Lisa Bevere
- *WomanCode* by Alisa Vitti

WEBSITES:

- The Marriage Bed
- Hot, Holy, and Humorous
- To Love, Honor, and Vacuum
- God Over Porn App
- XXXChurch
- Fight the New Drug
- AdoreMe (for lingerie)